THE ULTIMATE GUIDE FOR
STUDENT PRODUCT
DEVELOPMENT
& EVALUATION

THE ULTIMATE GUIDE FOR

STUDENT PRODUCT

DEVELOPMENT

& EVALUATION

SECOND EDITION

FRANCES A. KARNES, PH.D. & KRISTEN R. STEPHENS, PH.D.

PRUFROCK PRESS INC.
WACO, TEXAS

Library of Congress Cataloging-in-Publication Data

Karnes, Frances A.
  The ultimate guide for student product development & evaluation / Frances A. Karnes, Kristen R. Stephens. -- 2nd
ed.
      p. cm.
  Includes bibliographical references.
  ISBN-13: 978-1-59363-374-5 (pbk.)
  ISBN-10: 1-59363-374-2 (pbk.)
  1. Project method in teaching. I. Stephens, Kristen R. II. Title.
  LB1027.43.K37 2009
  371.3'6--dc22
                          2009019510

Edited by Lacy Compton
Production Design by Marjorie Parker

ISBN-13: 978-1-59363-374-5
ISBN-10: 1-59363-374-2

Prufrock Press Inc.
P.O. Box 8813
Waco, TX 76714-8813
Phone: (800) 998-2208
Fax: (800) 240-0333
http://www.prufrock.com

CONTENTS

ACKNOWLEDGEMENTS

To the many people who have made valuable contributions to this book, we extend our deepest appreciation. We are deeply indebted to the staff at the Frances A. Karnes Center for Gifted Studies at The University of Southern Mississippi and in the Program in Education at Duke University. To our administrators and colleagues at The University of Southern Mississippi and Duke University, we thank you for your support of this book and our other professional publications and endeavors.

INTRODUCTION

WHO WILL BENEFIT FROM THIS BOOK

Elementary and secondary school students are the focus of this book; however, there are many other audiences that will find the information contained here helpful. Teachers at all levels, across all subject areas, are encouraged to use this book to help facilitate student product development and evaluation. Guidance counselors, librarians, and media specialists also are sure to find many useful applications of this information. In addition, this book can be a valuable resource for organizations that serve youth in afterschool and summer programs.

HOW PRODUCTS WERE SELECTED FOR THIS BOOK

The products selected for this book were gleaned from many sources. Special attention was given to those products that further the development of 21st-century learning skills. The intent was to include as many products as possible that would appeal to a variety of learning styles and could be applied to a variety of disciplines. This edition of *The Ultimate Guide for Student Product Development & Evaluation* presents an entirely new set of 42 products, different than the 45 products presented in the previous edition. As with all human endeavors, a few products may have been overlooked, but we'll leave those for subsequent editions! The possibilities are limitless.

HOW TO USE THIS BOOK

This book is easy to use and has been divided into six chapters. Chapter 1 contains general information on the profiled products: definitions, types/categories, what you should know about their development, and the benefits of creating them. It also contains information on skills and standards met by completing the products.

Chapter 2 provides information on starting the product development process, including the formulation of a topic, the organization of product aspects, the transformation of content into products, the art and science of communicating ideas and knowledge through products, and the extremely necessary component of evaluation.

Considerations and methods for evaluating products are highlighted in Chapter 3. Strategies for developing rubrics, objectively assessing creativity, and monitoring group and collaborative product-producing endeavors are included.

Chapter 4 profiles the 42 selected products for this edition. An array of information is provided for each product, including a definition; career titles of the expert(s) best known for creating the product; the different types/variations of the product; terminology/vocabulary associated with the product; 21st-century skills addressed when creating the product; helpful hints to keep in mind when pursuing the development of the product; a listing of individuals who are deemed to be exemplary producers of the product; community resources, books, and Web sites where students can obtain additional information on the product; and inspirational quotes. Rubric starters for each product also are provided to guide the development of evaluation instruments for assessing students' products.

Chapter 5 profiles a variety of competitions that serve as venues for showcasing the products that students create. The volume concludes with a series of guided journal prompts located in Chapter 6 that afford students the opportunity to extend their reflection regarding the product development process.

WHAT IS A PRODUCT?

A product is tangible evidence of what has been learned through study and investigation. When a third-grade girl studies the economic concept of scarcity, she may want to demonstrate her understanding by doing one or all of the following: writing an editorial for the local newspaper, creating a video to be displayed in the mall, or developing a document to be shared with city economic developers. After researching the accomplishments of Mark Twain, a seventh-grade boy could write a script, create a stage set, and deliver a monologue to various groups of children and adults. These are but a few examples of how knowledge and understanding can be transformed into interesting products to be shared with a variety of audiences within the school and community.

Products are valuable, 21st-century tools for assessing student progress in that their development requires the application of new skills and concepts rather than just the retrieval of facts. Products help teachers determine the degree to which students understand and process new information, content, and concepts. Wiggins and McTighe (2005) indicated that products provide an "appropriate means of evoking and assessing enduring understandings" (p. 152).

TYPES OF PRODUCTS

There are many different types of products: written, oral, visual, performance, and multicategorical. Naturally, some types will be more appealing to particular students than others, and students often will gravitate toward those products that are aligned with their preferred learning styles. The goal should be to have students try their hand at a variety of different types of products, to ensure the development of a large repertoire of skills. A listing of possible products appears in Figure 1.

Abstract	Competition	Game show
Acronym	Computer document	Geocache
Activity sheet	Computer program	Geodesics
Advertisement	Conference presentation	Geometric model
Alphabet book	Construction	Glossary
Altered book	Cookbook	Graph
Animation	Cooked concoction	Graphic
Annotated bibliography	Costume	Graphic organizer
Aquarium	Crest	Greeting card
Archive	Critique	Guide
Art gallery	Cross section	Handbook
Audiotape	Crossword puzzle	Handout
Autobiography	Dance	Hidden picture
Ballad	Database	Histogram
Banner	Debate	Hologram
Bibliography	Demonstration	How-to book
Big book	Design	Hypermedia
Biography	Diagram	Hypothesis
Blog	Dialogue	Illuminated manuscript
Blueprint	Diary	Illusion
Board game	Dictionary	Illustrated story
Book	Digital story	Illustration
Book jacket	Diorama	Index cards
Book report	Display	Instructions
Book review	Document	Internet search
Booklet	Documentary	Interview
Bookmark	Doll	Invention
Broadcast	Dramatization	Investigation
Brochure	Drawing	Itinerary
Budget	Editorial	Jewelry
Bulletin board	Electronic scrapbook	Jigsaw puzzle
Bumper sticker	ePortfolio	Jingle
Business plan	Equation	Joke
Button	Essay	Journal
Calendar	Etching	Journal article
Campaign	Evaluation checklist	Journal entry
Cartoon	Event	Kit
Carving	Exhibit	Laser show
Catalog	Experiment	Law
Celebration	Fact file	Learning center
Characterization	Fairy tale	Lecture
Charade	Family tree	Lesson
Chart	Field experience	Letter
Checklist	Field guide	Limerick
Club	Film	List
Coat of arms	Finger puppet	Literary analysis
Collage	Flag	Log
Collection	Flannel board story	Logic puzzle
Coloring book	Flier	Logo
Comedy skit	Flip book	Machine
Comic strip	Flow chart	Magazine
Commemorative stamp	Folder game	Magazine article
Commentary	Fractal	Magic show
Commercial	Game	Manual

FIGURE 1. POSSIBLE PRODUCTS.

Manuscript	Picture dictionary	Shadow box
Map with key	Picture story	Shadow play
Mask	Pie chart	Short story
Matrix	Plan	Sign
Menu	Plaque	Silk screening
Metaphor	Play	Simulation
Mime	Podcast	Sketch
Mini-center	Poem	Skit
Mobile	Pointillism	Slide show
Mock interview	Political cartoon	Sociogram
Mock trial	Pop-up book	Song
Model	Portfolio	Speech
Monologue	Portrait	Spreadsheet
Montage	Position paper	Stage setting
Monument	Poster	Stained glass
Mosaic	PowerPoint	Stencil
Motto	Prediction	Stitchery
Multimedia presentation	Presentation	Story
Mural	Program	Storyboard
Museum	Project cube	Summary
Musical	Prototype	Survey
Musical composition	Puppet	Survival guide
Musical instrument	Puppet show	Table
Musical performance	Questionnaire	Tape recording
Mystery	Quilt	Television show
Myth	Quotations	Terrarium
Narrative	Radio show	Tessellation
Needlecraft	Rap	Test
Newsletter	Rebus story	Textbook
Newspaper	Recipe	Theory
Newspaper article	Recitation	Three-dimensional model
Novel	Recording	Time capsule
Oral report	Reenactment	Timeline
Organization	Reflection	Toy
Origami	Relief map	Trademark
Ornament	Report	Travelogue
Outline	Resume	Triptych
Overhead transparency	Riddle	Venn diagram
Packet	Role-play	Video
Painting	Routine	Video game
Pamphlet	Rubber stamp	Virtual field trip
Panel discussion	Rubbing	Virtual museum
Pantomime	Rubric	Vocabulary list
Papier mâché	Samples	Wall hanging
Pattern	Sand casting	Watercolor
Performance	Scavenger hunt	Weaving
Personal experience	Scenario	Web page
Petition	Science fiction story	Webbing
Photo album	Scrapbook	Webinar
Photo essay	Script	WebQuest
Photojournalism	Sculpture	Wiki
Photograph	Self-portrait	Woodworking
Pictograph	Seminar	Word puzzle
Pictorial essay	Service project	Written paper

FIGURE 1. POSSIBLE PRODUCTS.

FACTORS TO CONSIDER IN PRODUCT DEVELOPMENT

Deciding on a type of product to display the knowledge gained from the topic can be a difficult task. Kettle, Renzulli, and Rizza (1998) have devised My Way . . . An Expression Style Inventory. This instrument can be used to gather information about the types of products that students may be interested in creating. This inventory divides products into 10 different categories: written, oral, artistic, computer, audio-visual, commercial, service, dramatization, manipulative, and musical. By answering a series of questions on a Likert-type scale, it can be determined which sort of product would be of greatest interest. Other ways to select a product type might be accomplished by completing an interest inventory or generating a list of hobbies and strengths.

An online assessment of interests, learning style, and product preference is available through the Renzulli Learning System (http://www.renzullilearning.com). Schools can purchase site licenses to access the system. Students simply login and complete a questionnaire to assess their interests, learning styles, and product preferences. Personalized enrichment experiences (e.g., virtual field trips, books, research opportunities) are then provided based on each student's profile. Teachers have access to student profiles and can use this information to easily group students by interest, learning style, and product preference. Parents also can access their child's profile and can be assured that the Web sites their child is visiting are safe and recommended by educational experts.

LEARNING STYLES

The learning styles of individuals vary and should be considered when engaging in product development. For students with advanced art skills, visual products may be preferred. For those with outstanding writing abilities, products emphasizing writing often will be pursued. After a student becomes comfortable developing the types of products most suited to his or her learning style and/or strength area, the exploration of other product formats should be encouraged to ensure that students develop a broad range of skills.

AUDIENCE

The audience with whom the product will be shared also should be considered when deciding on an appropriate product to communicate information. Although an editorial addressing the need for more stringent water conservation regulations would be appropriate for older students and adults, a puppet show conveying the same concept/issue would be better suited to an audience of elementary school students.

SUBJECT MATTER

Considering which type of product is best suited to display the selected subject matter is crucial. For instance, students will have to decide whether a graph, diorama, play, multimedia slideshow, or another product would best display the stages of metamorphosis. Although all may be appropriate, deciding which one best conveys the content can be challenging.

MATERIAL AVAILABILITY

Another factor to consider in product development is the availability of materials. Are all readily available? Are the costs of needed materials within reason? Although some products can be developed using standard consumable supplies typically found in every classroom (i.e., paper, paints, glue, etc.), others require the acquisition of more atypical equipment and materials (i.e., diode laser, video editing software, pliers, wire, etc.). In order to ensure that supplies and materials are on hand, a list such as the one in Figure 2 can be sent home to parents, grandparents, and friends so that desired items can be donated.

Lack of adequate resources can curtail the development of many products, but with some creative problem solving and determination, this obstacle can be surmounted.

TIME

Perhaps one of the biggest constraints on a teacher's ability to employ creative product development in the classroom is time. In an era of high-stakes testing and accountability, many teachers feel pressure to cover as much content as possible in order to prepare students for end-of-grade tests. Product development can be time intensive, and many teachers are uncertain about how to effectively incorporate such experiences for students into the existing school schedule. However, it is important to note that product development aligns with many of the state and national competency goals across disciplines. Additionally, the development of products requires learners to engage with content and concepts at a higher level through analysis, synthesis, and evaluation. Products are a 21st-century assessment tool and must be utilized to prepare future-ready students; therefore, teachers are encouraged to consider product development as an essential rather than a superfluous component of the curriculum.

RISK-TAKING

It is important for teachers to encourage students to explore a variety of products. Figure 3 provides a method of tracking the types of products individual students develop over time, so students can be redirected as needed. This form can follow students as they advance through school. By encouraging

Don't Throw It Away!

Aluminum foil	Costume jewelry	Paints & brushes
Beads	Egg cartons	Paper scraps
Berry baskets	Fabric scraps	Ribbon & yarn
Boxes	Greeting cards	Sponges
Butter tubs	Milk cartons	Wire
Buttons	Newspapers	Wire coat hangers
Cans	Nuts, bolts, screws	Wood scraps
Cardboard tubes	Old keys	Wrapping paper
Clothespins	Old magazines	Yogurt cups
	Packaging popcorn	

FIGURE 2. LIST OF ITEMS THAT CAN BE DONATED FOR PRODUCT MATERIALS.

Student Name:_____

Date	Type of Product	Academic Subject	Grade Level/Teacher

FIGURE 3. STUDENT PRODUCT INVENTORY.

students to develop a type of product that may be out of their comfort zone, they become engaged in healthy risk taking. Neihart (1999) suggested that such intellectual risk taking helps to "increase self-esteem, confidence, and courage in gifted youth" (p. 289). Challenging students' limitations is necessary to foster high levels of achievement and leadership (Neihart, 1999).

STUDENT DISPOSITIONS

Before students can successfully engage in product development, they must have a disposition that encourages and allows for effective problem solving. If students do not enter the product development experience with the essential skills and mindset, the outcomes expected by teachers may not be achieved.

The fundamental goal of product development should be to help students *produce* new knowledge and ideas rather than *reproduce* or regurgitate existing knowledge. In order for students to successfully achieve this endeavor, they must possess the dispositions and attributes necessary to approach, think about, and resolve problems.

Costa and Kallick (2000) described 16 Habits of Mind that must be developed and employed by students for new knowledge and ideas to incubate and thrive. These 16 attributes follow with details regarding how each are specifically related to creative product development.

1. *Persisting.* Students must be able to stick to a task until it is completed. When developing products that require an extended focus and time commitment, some students may be too quick to abandon their efforts before completion. Other students may become frustrated when their product is not turning out how they initially envisioned and resort to haphazardly throwing something together so they can be done with it. Students must be encouraged to employ alternative strategies in problem solving when their initial methods fail. Knowing how to approach and sustain the problem-solving process over time is a fundamental skill in maintaining persistence.

2. *Managing Impulsivity.* Before students dive headfirst into developing their product, they must have a vision and a plan of action that details their goal. Teaching students how to slow down and effectively reflect on each alternative and consequence also will help eliminate the number of errors along the way.

3. *Listening to Others—With Understanding and Empathy.* Many products that students will create in the classroom are the result of a group rather than individual effort. Students need to develop skills in group dynamics and become astute in listening, understanding, and considering the perspectives of others. Such skills will allow students to build upon each other's ideas, resulting in a more sophisticated and complex product.

4. *Thinking Flexibly.* In order to produce creative products, students must be willing to explore various perspectives and approach problems from

different angles. Flexible thinking also requires students to consider and ponder various points of a problem, avoid making a rush judgment, and tolerate ambiguity.

5. *Thinking About Our Thinking (Metacognition).* Perhaps one of the most beneficial aspects of creative product development is the mental processes that are developed while students are engaged in the activity of production. Through each stage of the process students are planning, reflecting, and monitoring their progress toward established goals. Students need to be encouraged to think about the mental processes they are using as they work through the steps of a problem and how these steps and their sequence might be altered to improve performance.

6. *Striving for Accuracy and Precision.* Many times students strive for expedience rather than excellence. It is important for students to learn to value the craftsmanship of their work. The finished product should meet predetermined criteria and be of a quality similar to professionals.

7. *Questioning and Posing Problems.* In order to produce new knowledge, students must be able to ask effective and relevant questions. Teachers can help develop student questioning skills by modeling intriguing questioning in the classroom. Questions need to engage students so they want to put forth the effort in attempting to answer them. A good question is essential to the research and creative product development process.

8. *Applying Past Knowledge to New Situations.* Students should be encouraged to make connections between new and past knowledge. Teachers can aid this process by making both inter- and intradisciplinary connections with the content being taught. Helping students assimilate new ideas with existing knowledge fosters greater retention and understanding. Connections within and across disciplines also help students consider content in creative and novel ways.

9. *Thinking and Communicating With Clarity and Precision.* When students develop products with an audience in mind, they must consider the best methods for explaining their knowledge and ideas to others. Presenting their products to authentic audiences also helps students build communication skills.

10. *Gathering Data Through All Senses.* The act of creating a product allows students to utilize a variety of senses, both within and outside of their preferred learning style. The opportunity to manipulate materials and actively engage with the content enhances understanding.

11. *Creating, Imagining, and Innovating.* Through creative product development, students are able to generate original ideas and strive for improvement by eliciting and welcoming constructive feedback of their work. Students also must have the flexibility to fine-tune and explore their ideas in greater depth.

12. *Responding With Wonderment and Awe.* When students engage in product development they are able to explore the problems they are most

passionate about. Teachers can model lifelong learning for their students by encouraging curiosity, enthusiasm, and inquiry in the classroom.

13. *Taking Responsible Risks.* Some students may be reluctant to take risks in their product development. For example, they may stick with creating those products for which they have experienced the most success. Teachers should encourage students to take intellectual risks by delving into new, uncertain areas. Students are more likely to experience growth if they try out new ideas and products rather than just stick to what is safe. Students should welcome new challenges.

14. *Finding Humor.* Through product development, students must convey their information and ideas to others. Knowing when and if the incorporation of humor is appropriate to the topic and tone of a presentation is vital to the creative problem-solving process. In addition, teachers can help students learn to laugh at mistakes they make and to appreciate that human error is a fundamental part of the learning process. Humor also can help alleviate the stress that some students may feel as they engage in the product development process—particularly anxiety related to presenting in front of an audience.

15. *Thinking Interdependently.* Interaction with others can greatly enhance a learning experience. Whether a student is working independently or in a group, the activity of bouncing ideas off others can help refine and shape one's thoughts. Product development should be a social event in the classroom. Even if students are each working on their own projects, teachers still can encourage students to illicit suggested strategies and feedback from their peers along the way.

16. *Learning Continuously.* Even after a product has been created, a grade assigned, and a new topic introduced, students can continue to reflect and act on the ideas generated from the product development process. Teachers should encourage students to continue to explore alternatives and refine their solutions, as this is the essence of inquiry. (Stephens & Karnes, 2009, pp. 159–161)

Introducing and nurturing these dispositions in the classroom provides the foundation needed for successful product development in the classroom.

BENEFITS OF PRODUCT DEVELOPMENT

The potential benefits of product development on student learning are great. Several key areas of student growth and development can be addressed through the implementation of product development in the classroom.

HIGH-LEVEL THINKING

Paper-and-pencil tasks frequently are used to assess students' *knowledge* and *comprehension* of the content, which are low-level thought processes. Product development can deepen and extend student understanding in a content area by requiring engagement at higher cognitive levels. In addition, the relevancy of subject matter is enhanced, inter- and intradisciplinary connections are forged, and essential concepts of a discipline are more readily retained when students engage in product development.

PROCESS SKILLS

A multitude of process skills also are developed during product development. These include, but are not limited to, skills in oral and written communication, creativity, critical thinking, and research. The organizational skills of planning, record keeping, and time management are enhanced through product development. Also, when working with others, aspects of group dynamics such as teamwork, decision making, communication, and consensus building can be further developed.

21ST-CENTURY KNOWLEDGE AND SKILLS

Preparing future-ready learners has become a central theme embedded in educational reform initiatives. So, what are 21st-century skills? How are such skills taught and assessed? What can teachers and schools do to ensure that all students graduate prepared for a 21st-century workforce?

The Partnership for 21st Century Skills (http://www.21stcenturyskills.org) is an advocacy organization focused on infusing 21st-century skills into education. The partnership has identified outcomes (skills, knowledge, and expertise) that should be required of students in the 21st century. These outcomes include:

- global awareness;
- financial, economic, and/or business literacy;
- entrepreneurial literacy;
- civic literacy;
- health literacy;
- creativity and innovation skills;
- critical thinking and problem-solving skills;
- communication skills;
- collaboration skills;
- information literacy;
- media literacy;
- technology skills;
- flexibility and adaptability;
- initiative and self-direction;

- social and cross-cultural skills;
- productivity and accountability;
- leadership and responsibility;
- interdisciplinary understanding; and
- mastery of core subjects, including:
  - English, reading, or language arts;
  - world languages;
  - arts;
  - mathematics;
  - economics;
  - science;
  - geography;
  - history; and
  - government and civics.

The expectation is that students will gain a deep understanding of high-level content and its interconnectedness with 21st-century themes (see above list for themes). In addition to thinking skills, and a deep understanding of a subject, there also are several essential life and career skills that will be needed by students. These include flexibility and adaptability, initiative and self-direction, social and cross-cultural skills, productivity and accountability, and leadership and responsibility (which almost mirror the Habits of Mind proposed by Costa and Kallick [2000]).

From these identified 21st-century skills, it is evident that a balanced focus between developing cognitive and social skills is essential as schools prepare 21st-century learners. Although there appear to be many available methods for assessing basic knowledge and skills in the content areas, there is still much to learn regarding how to assess those applied skills needed for the 21st century. High-quality standardized testing paired with effective classroom assessments are critical to monitor student mastery and growth, and new assessment tools that specifically analyze 21st-century skills must be developed. Most tests measure students' knowledge of isolated facts, not their ability to apply such knowledge in real-world contexts. Based on the complexity and number of competencies encompassing 21st-century knowledge and skills, no singular instrument will suffice. Instead, a menu of assessment tools must be made available, and product development can and should serve as one valuable piece of the assessment puzzle.

Along with student outcomes, the partnership also has identified support systems that must be in place to ensure that students master 21st-century skills. This support system includes 21st century:

1. standards,
2. assessments,
3. curriculum and instruction,
4. professional development, and
5. learning environments.

All of these support systems have direct implications for product development in the classroom:

1. Product development engages students with authentic data and tools to solve meaningful problems. As a result, students develop deep, rather than surface, understandings within a discipline. (Standards)
2. Products can serve as a multidimensional assessment tool as they provide teachers with a method for simultaneously evaluating content mastery; learning and innovation skills (e.g., critical thinking, problem solving); information, media, and technology skills (e.g., information literacy); and life and career skills (e.g., flexibility, initiative, responsibility). (Assessments)
3. Product development supports innovative teaching and learning methods that integrate technology, problem-based learning, and higher order thinking skills. Product development also encourages the integration of community resources and extends learning beyond the classroom into the community. (Curriculum and instruction)
4. To prepare 21st-century learners, teachers will have to carefully evaluate the impact of their teaching methods in the classroom and determine which learning environments best promote 21st-century skills. As a result of this analysis, it is likely that certain practices may be replaced or de-emphasized in order to achieve a better balance between direct teaching approaches and project-oriented methods. The incorporation of product development into the classroom can help achieve this balance and also can better address the needs of diverse learners by providing them with alternate forums to demonstrate progress. (Professional development)
5. Through product development, students learn in relevant, real-world, 21st-century contexts that afford them the opportunity to engage in both individual and group-based projects. (Learning environments)

CURRICULUM STANDARDS

It previously was noted that creative product development affords students the opportunity to practice and apply 21st-century skills and competencies. Such skills are vital in preparing students for the workforce they will encounter upon graduation. In addition, through product development, students can demonstrate competency across disciplines, as products provide a venue by which conceptual understanding and content knowledge can be authentically applied and assessed. Furthermore, unlike tests and paper-and-pencil worksheets, products fully engage students with the content and concepts they are exploring, affording them the opportunity to immediately apply what they are learning rather than simply regurgitating isolated facts and information outside of a relevant context. As a result, through the development of creative products, there is a greater likelihood that students will retain the information learned, understand its application to the real world, and make valid connections within and between disciplines.

In exploring the essential standards of the various disciplines, it is evident that there are many rich and meaningful applications of creative problem development that can be used to address established curriculum standards. The following sections provide excerpts from the national standards of the core disciplines. These excerpts further speak to the need to incorporate product development into the classroom and are offered to help teachers see that creative product development is not an "add-on" to the curriculum, but is a valuable essential that can and should be embedded into the curriculum across all grade levels. Keep in mind that these are but a few of the many statements presented within the national standards that align with product development. Key concepts/terms derived from the excerpt also are listed for emphasis.

Excerpt From *Curriculum Standards for Social Studies*

Social studies teaching and learning are powerful when they are active:
- Students develop new understanding through a process of active construction of knowledge.
- Teachers gradually move from providing considerable guidance by modeling, explaining, or supplying information that builds student knowledge, to a less directive role that encourages students to become independent and self-regulated learners.
- Powerful social studies teaching emphasizes authentic activities that call for real-life applications using the skills and content of the field. (National Council for Social Studies, n.d., para. 50)

Key concepts that teachers should take from this excerpt include the importance of active construction, independent and self-regulated learners, authentic activities, and real-life applications of content.

Excerpt From the *National Science Education Standards*

Developing Student Abilities and Understanding:
From the earliest grades, students should experience science in a form that engages them in the active construction of ideas and explanations and enhances their opportunities to develop the abilities of doing science. Teaching science as inquiry provides teachers with the opportunity to develop student abilities and to enrich student understanding of science. Students should do science in ways that are within their developmental capabilities. (National Research Council, 1996, p. 121)

Key concepts that teachers should take from this excerpt include the value of experience, active construction, doing, and inquiry.

Excerpt From *Principles and Standards for School Mathematics*

> The Learning Principle
> Learning with understanding also helps students become autonomous learners. Students learn more and better when they take control of their own learning. When challenged with appropriately chosen tasks, students can become confident in their ability to tackle difficult problems, eager to figure things out on their own, flexible in exploring mathematical ideas, and willing to persevere when tasks are challenging. (National Council of Teachers of Mathematics, 2000, para. 4)

Key concepts that teachers should take from this excerpt include the importance of autonomous learners and perseverance and the ability of students to take control of their own learning and figure things out on their own.

Excerpt From *Standards for the English Language Arts*

> Standard 7: Students conduct research on issues and interests by generating ideas and questions, and by posing problems. They gather, evaluate, and synthesize data from a variety of sources (e.g., print and nonprint texts, artifacts, people) to communicate their discoveries in ways that suit their purpose and audience.
>
> It is essential that students acquire a wide range of abilities and tools for raising questions, investigating concerns, and solving problems . . .
>
> Students need to learn creative and multifaceted approaches to research and inquiry. The ability to identify good topics, to gather information, and to evaluate, assemble, and interpret findings from among the many general and specialized information sources now available to them is one of the most vital skills that students can acquire. (National Council of Teachers of English, 1996, pp. 27–28)

Key concepts that teachers should take from this excerpt include the value of students raising questions, participating in investigations, problem solving, and evaluating and interpreting findings.

STAGES OF PRODUCT DEVELOPMENT

There are several stages students go through when creating a product. These stages are:
1. formulation of a topic,
2. organization of production aspects,
3. transformation of content,
4. communication through products,
5. evaluation,
6. celebration, and
7. reflection.

FORMULATION OF A TOPIC

The first stage in developing a product is selecting a topic to investigate. Topics can be content-specific, such as pirates, Egypt, wolves, or architecture, or they can be more conceptual such as freedom, leadership, change, or cultures. Following are some strategies students should keep in mind when selecting a topic to explore.

Narrow the Focus

It is important for students to narrow the topic from broad to specific. For example, the topic of astronomy might be focused on the Big Dipper or black holes. Constructing a web, such as the one in Figure 4, can assist in this process. A more narrowly focused topic makes the research process more manageable.

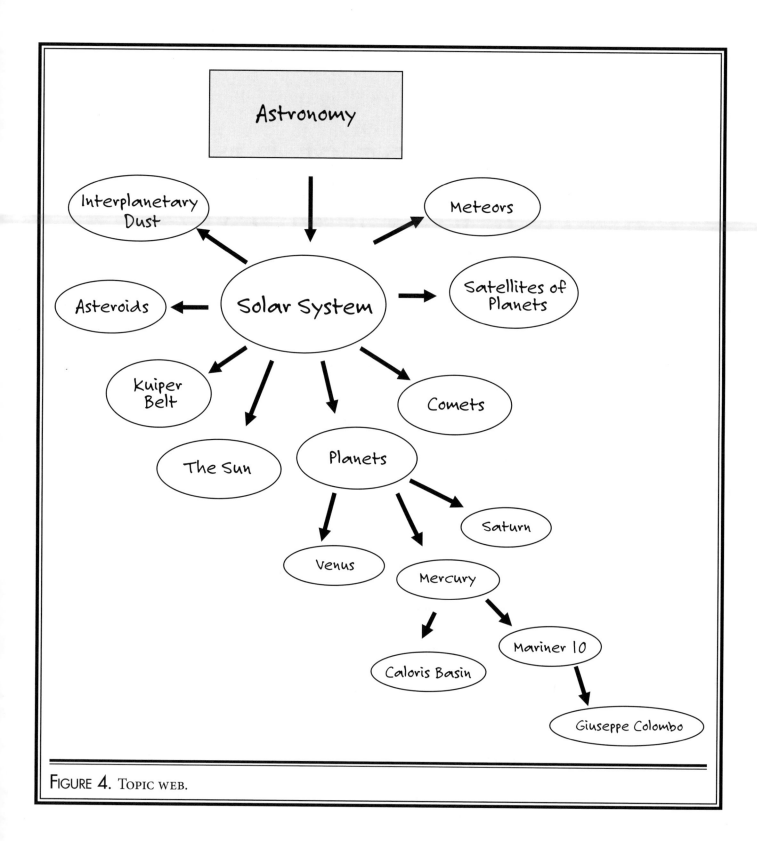

FIGURE 4. TOPIC WEB.

BUILD NEW KNOWLEDGE

Students should be encouraged to select a topic from which they can learn and grow. If a student has read every book about tornadoes and already has developed several products pertaining to tornadoes, he or she should select a different topic from which new knowledge can be gained.

SELECT AN AREA OF INTEREST

Students should choose topics in which they have a genuine interest. This will serve as a motivator for the student to carry out product development to completion. Those who have been interested in tornadoes, for example, might find the topic of hurricanes fascinating as well.

CONSULT MULTIPLE SOURCES

Students must research their topic using a variety of sources, including books, encyclopedias, the Internet, films, interviews, newspapers, authentic documents, atlases, experiments, and so forth. The goal is to seek a variety of perspectives on the topic. It also is advisable to select a topic for which resources are available. Resources that can be used to gather information related to choosing a topic include:

- *Periodicals*: journals, magazines, newsletters, newspapers;
- *Books*: content-specific, encyclopedias, manuals, reference;
- *Audio-Visual Media*: computer software, podcasts, television programs, video/DVDs, Webinar/Voice Over Internet Protocol (VOIP), Web sites; and
- *Miscellaneous*: dissertations/theses, e-mails, letters, meetings/symposiums, memos, monographs, personal communication, primary source documents, reports, unpublished manuscripts.

INFORMATION LITERACY

Students should be able to determine which sources of information are credible. Although the Internet provides a wealth of resources, it also contains information that is inaccurate and biased. For example, the online encyclopedia Wikipedia (http://www.wikipedia.com) has become quite popular with students; however, the site itself acknowledges that "significant misinformation, unencyclopedic content, or vandalism" (Wikipedia, 2007, para. 3) may exist in newer entries.

ORGANIZATION OF PRODUCTION ASPECTS

The second phase, the organization stage, runs the length of the product developing experience. Several organizational techniques can be utilized to help keep students focused and provide structure to daily activities related to product development. A well-developed organizational plan teaches students the necessity of setting and achieving both short- and long-term goals. Organizational skills need to be taught and can benefit students in a variety of academic endeavors. Following are some suggested organizational techniques that can be applied by students.

CALENDARS AND TIMELINES

Daily activities may be placed on a calendar to build time-management skills. This strategy helps students stay on task and allows them to visualize an end to their means. Furthermore, students should reflect on their accomplishments at the end of each day and evaluate progress toward meeting their established goals. By staying organized and working toward a projected date, students demonstrate the ability to be responsible for their own learning.

LOGS

Students can record daily progress and set an agenda for the next day in a project log. This approach encourages students to consider in advance the materials they will need to bring to class to complete their product. Logs can be kept in a spiral notebook or on a special form, which can be designed by the teacher or student. Such forms may require students to answer questions pertaining to current progress and future plans. Figure 5 provides an example of information that may be kept in a daily log.

RESEARCH READINESS

Research readiness refers to the organizational activities that precede the research process. Research readiness can include:
- generating a list of questions pertaining to the topic to guide research;
- developing a KWL chart (What I Know, What I Want to Know, What I Learned; see Figure 6 for an example); and
- producing a list of resources where the answers to formulated research questions might be found.

Students may be engaged in more than one research endeavor at a time. It is essential for them not only to conduct research about the topic they are investigating, but also to conduct research regarding the development of their product. For example, a student researching the roles of women in ancient Egypt will

MY PRODUCT LOG

Name: Date:

Product: Topic:

What I accomplished today:

My plans for the next work session:

Materials and resources I will need for the next work session:

ESTIMATED COMPLETION DATE

☐ Is still: ☐ Needs to be changed to:

                                         Reason(s) for change:

Student signature:

Teacher signature:

FIGURE 5. PRODUCT LOG.

Know	**W**ant to Know	**L**earned
• Soil is all around us. • Worms like to live in soil. • Plants need soil to grow. • When soil gets wet it becomes mud. • Soil looks different in different places. • Dirt is another word for soil.	• Why does some soil look and feel different than others? • What other kinds of animals live in the soil? • How is soil made?	• Soil is made of sand, silt, and clay. The amount of each of these substances determines the texture and appearance of the soil. • Slugs, snails, bacteria, and moles also live in soil. • Soil is made from eroded rocks and minerals and decaying plant and animal matter called humus.

FIGURE 6. SAMPLE KWL CHART FOR SOIL UNIT.

be reading books and surfing the Internet for information regarding Egyptian women during this period. If the student has selected to design a costume that is representative of what Egyptian women wore, then he or she also may be reading books and interviewing costume designers to gather information about fabrics, patterns, sewing techniques, and so forth. Essentially, two different types of research are going on simultaneously: research to gather content knowledge and research to gather product knowledge.

DETERMINING AUDIENCES

Before students decide what type of product will best convey their new knowledge, it is essential that they create a list of possible audiences with whom to share their products. Audiences both inside and outside of school should be considered. The characteristics of the audience, along with the information to be shared, will greatly influence the type and complexity of the product selected. Possible audiences might include peers, community leaders, younger students, retirement communities, the school board, clubs, and so forth.

PRODUCT SELECTION

Once the audience and presentation content have been selected, students can determine which type of product will be most suitable. Media are the mode through which ideas are communicated. Selecting appropriate forms of media may be a complicated step for some students. They often tend to select media that reflect their particular learning style. As mentioned previously, authors will write and artists will illustrate. Sometimes, the medium that will best demonstrate, represent, or symbolize an idea may not be the one the student normally would have selected. Keeping a list of possible products, as found in Figure 1, may help students choose varied media that will communicate their ideas, thoughts, and concepts most effectively.

MATERIAL GATHERING

Once the product type has been selected, students should generate a list of materials needed to complete the proposed products. Accommodations for certain materials due to expense and availability may need to be considered. These adjustments require students to utilize their creative problem-solving abilities in authentic situations. Furthermore, materials that students first thought were appropriate may not work as planned. Through substitution and experimentation with alternate materials, they will enhance their problem-solving abilities and practice a valuable life skill—flexibility.

EVALUATION CRITERIA

Before creating their product, students should develop criteria for evaluating the finished piece. By establishing criteria for evaluation early on, students are made aware of the standards to which they aspire.

Students may consult with an expert in the topic field for assistance in developing a list of components and exemplary characteristics for the proposed product. For example, a cartographer or geography professor may be an excellent resource for a student who desires to create a map; a genealogist would provide information related to the components and characteristics of an ideal family tree; and a local reporter may offer advice on how to conduct a professional quality interview. Baker and Schacter (1996) suggested using adult expert performance as a benchmark for assessment. In addition, Wiggins (1996) suggested that teachers look for "exemplars" or "anchors," or examples of a particular product that demonstrate an exceptional standard. These exemplars can serve as a basis for setting performance standards for students. The following is a suggested list of specific products with the experts that may be consulted when developing evaluation criteria:

blueprint	→	architect
brochure	→	marketing consultant
debate	→	speech-debate teacher
exhibit	→	museum curator
experiment	→	scientist
family tree	→	genealogist
magazine	→	editor
map	→	cartographer or geographer
musical composition	→	music professor
photograph	→	photographer
play	→	actor or professor of theater
sculpture	→	local artist
Web page	→	Webmaster

Experts are everywhere. Many can be found in your local community through the following sources:

- colleges and universities,
- businesses,
- clubs and organizations,
- friends,
- craft guilds,
- local media,
- the Internet,
- the telephone directory, and
- the library.

The Internet provides a valuable source of experts if they cannot be found within your community. For instance, students can send questions related to a specific discipline to experts in that field. Additional "Ask an Expert" Web sites can be found by discipline by using an Internet search engine.

TRANSFORMATION OF CONTENT

Because the attainment of higher level thinking skills is essential for future readiness, the type of products expected from students should be highly creative and perhaps abstract. Products should represent more than the mere acquisition of new knowledge. They should convey a genuine application of synthesis and analysis. This process of transformation allows the student to turn new knowledge into something more meaningful. Maker and Nielson (1996) outlined several elements of transformation: viewing from a different perspective, reinterpreting, elaborating, extending, and combining simultaneously. When evaluating a product, it is important to look for some of these elements in students' work. Students should turn learned content into their own creation instead of repeating or summarizing general information. Forster (1990) described the process of project development as "the act of surprising oneself with new ideas" (p. 40). The ultimate goal of product development is to transform student research on a topic/concept into new thoughts, ideas, and perspectives.

Transformation involves many steps and processes. Students should be taught these steps and the types of activities associated with each as they move through the process. The steps include:

1. *Research:* The student locates, comprehends, and classifies information in order to gain knowledge.
2. *Information filtration:* The student processes, interprets, refines, and extrapolates the knowledge and ideas gained from research.
3. *Idea generation:* From the selected information, the student analyzes various elements, concepts, and ideas of interest.
4. *Centralization:* The student selects, decides, and focuses on a specific element or idea.
5. *Reflection:* The student considers, ponders, and judges the selected idea.
6. *Manipulation:* The student tests and experiments with the idea and changes, improves, and adapts it as necessary.
7. *Execution:* The student decides, organizes, prepares, and produces a product to display the idea.
8. *Communication:* The student shares, performs, displays, or disseminates the product to an authentic audience.

A model of the above transformation process appears in Figure 7. It is important to note the percentage of time students are spending in each phase of the transformation model. Typically, students spend little time planning and dive into the actual creation of their product. How often have students been observed with a fresh piece of poster board and a box of markers getting to work immediately without planning, sketching a draft, or constructing a prototype? How would the quality of what they are able to produce be impacted if more time and consideration were devoted to these initial steps?

As previously mentioned, the steps in the transformation model should be taught to students, and each phase should receive ample time and consideration. Perhaps one of the first goals in fostering successful product development in students is teaching them how to slow down and think and plan prior to acting. When introducing the model, it is suggested that the teacher initially designate an amount of time to be spent by students at each step (e.g., three class periods for investigation, two class periods for information filtration). However, keep in mind that, depending on the complexity and depth of the topic being researched, time periods for each step may vary. Spending a thorough amount of time researching and reflecting on the topic will help students generate novel ideas. Otherwise, they will likely resort to a mere regurgitation of what they read from a book—which is not transformation.

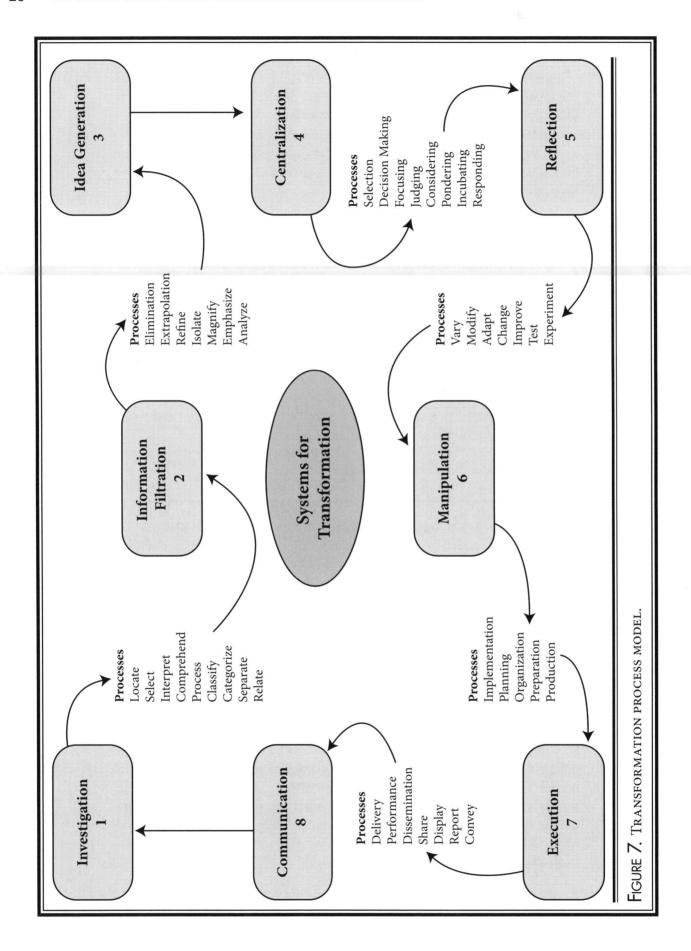

FIGURE 7. TRANSFORMATION PROCESS MODEL.

The transformation model easily can be adapted for use with younger students. Teachers can rename each step and provide further elaboration so that younger students have a better understanding of the type of activities that need to be occurring along the way. For example:

- explore the topic in depth (investigation),
- determine what is important (information filtration),
- record your thoughts and ideas (idea generation),
- decide which idea you like best (centralization),
- think about your idea overnight (reflection),
- develop a draft or prototype (manipulation),
- design your product (execution), and
- share the results (communication).

COMMUNICATION THROUGH PRODUCTS

During the communication stage, students share their ideas and products with a selected audience. Sharing the final product with an audience gives added purpose to the product. Instead of being stored in the back of a closet to collect dust, student products can provide valuable learning opportunities for many types of audiences.

Speaking Skills

Speaking skills will be enhanced through the continued exposure to a wide variety of audiences. Eye contact, clear speech, and confidence are a few components of an effective presentation. Students should become more comfortable with practice and experience in presenting their products and ideas. Never assume that a student who is unable to give an effective presentation has not synthesized and analyzed information from his or her study. Presenting the product in class should be the first step, followed by audiences within the school and community. Younger students will need time to feel comfortable expressing themselves in front of others. It is advisable to keep audiences small and familiar for younger students until they build confidence presenting to larger, more unfamiliar groups.

OTHER SHARING SHOWCASES

Products also can be attractively displayed in many areas throughout the community. This gives a sense of pride and importance to the student while serving as a great public relations tool by introducing the excitement and learning being generated in the community's classrooms. Some places that student products may be displayed in your community include:

- airports,
- bank lobbies,
- business offices,
- clubs and organizations,
- colleges and universities,
- fairs or festivals,
- government offices,
- hospitals,
- libraries,
- magazines,
- malls,
- newsletters,
- newspapers,
- post offices,
- preschools,
- PTA meetings,
- real estate offices,
- restaurants,
- retirement communities,
- school administrative offices,
- school board meetings,
- stores,
- town halls,
- train and bus stations, and
- Web sites.

Students also may choose to enter their products in a competition. Information related to specific academic areas, as well as fine and performing arts, leadership, and service learning, can be found in Chapter 5 and also in *Competitions for Talented Kids* (Karnes & Riley, 2005). The possibilities of potential audiences and display areas are abundant.

EVALUATION

Evaluation of student products should be multidimensional so that students can receive helpful and extensive feedback from a wide array of sources. Assessment may be determined by the teacher using preselected criteria, self-evaluation by the students, and feedback from an audience. Forster (1990) suggested that projects should have self-regulatory and constant evaluation methods so that students can stay on course throughout the duration of the project. Students may wish to develop questionnaires to determine their audiences' perceptions of their products and presentations. Before beginning their projects, it also is advisable that students choose a support person with whom they can conference periodically to share progress and receive feedback. Gibbons (1991) suggested that this support person be an expert in the particular topic, if possible.

ESTABLISHING CRITERIA

Students should be involved in establishing the criteria for product evaluation. If students are familiar with the criteria prior to beginning work, they will be more apt to produce successful products. Establishing criteria for evaluating products that are complex in nature can be difficult. Byrnes and Parke (1982) developed the Creative Products Scale, an easy-to-use scale for creative products such as drama, poetry, music, and dance. The scale contains glossaries of the important components of these unique products, making them easy for students and teachers to use effectively. As mentioned previously, topic experts also can be asked to assist in developing criteria for certain products. Renzulli, Reis, and Smith (1981) developed the Student Product Assessment Form, which rates eight factors in product development: purpose; problem focusing; level of resources; diversity of resources; appropriateness of resources; logic, sequence, and transition; action orientation; and audience.

When each student in a class is engaged in developing a different product, the task of evaluating each one can overwhelm teachers. How does one evaluate a diorama, a skit, or an illustration objectively? Therefore, getting students involved in the process of developing an effective evaluation instrument is crucial. It not only assists them in developing goals and criteria for the anticipated outcome, but it also holds them accountable for working toward and meeting these goals. Rubrics can be designed for every type of product, an entire class can create a rubric together, or students can develop their own rubrics specific to their product.

As mentioned earlier, evaluation of student products should be multidimensional, which can be achieved by having a variety of evaluators. These might include peers, audience members, teachers, the student, topic experts, or school administrators.

CELEBRATION

What better motivator to work diligently and produce a high-quality product than to have the chance to celebrate and reflect upon your accomplishments? Gibbons (1991) suggested that students have a party and share their products with one another informally, which allows them to see the wide variety of products they are capable of producing. Students can share the thought processes that went into designing their products and perhaps even have the opportunity to explore the topic further, as more questions are generated when minds meet.

Celebration is an important component of product development. It allows students to build confidence and feel good about their achievements. A product fair can provide students with the opportunity to share their products in a completely different type of stress-free setting. Renzulli and Reis (1991) suggested an end-of-year product fair, which includes coverage by local newspapers and television and radio stations. Such coverage would expand the students' audience and provide excellent public relations for the gifted program. Through such an event students also can share the stages in the development, implementation, and evaluation of their products.

REFLECTION

As students pack up their products on the bus and depart for home, the time for reflection begins. They should be encouraged to reflect on the entire process of creating their product from beginning to end. Is there anything else about the topic that needs further research? What could have been done differently? What really worked? These reflections will be a valuable contribution toward improvement as students begin a new journey into another product frontier. They will learn from both their successes and failures. In a sense, they will learn a great deal about themselves and others. Often, people reflect on things without even realizing it, but, by purposely doing so, a great deal can be learned that will be of value in the future.

Reflection also is a skill that needs to be taught. John Dewey (1933) recognized that it is not the experience but the reflection on the experience that leads to learning. Too often this stage in product development is overlooked, but it is essential that adequate time be provided for students to reflect.

One method students can use to reflect on their product producing experience is keeping a detailed journal. This will help them keep track of the steps of product development and also will serve as a way for them to remember and reflect on the entire process. Students will have gained an abundance of new knowledge through their research, planning, and creative problem-solving experiences.

Careful planning and organization are important components of successful product development. In addition to the suggestions given, a form such as the one displayed in Figure 8 can be used to keep a record of the various planning stages.

PRODUCT PLANNER

Name:

Date:

Product:

Topic:

Description and components of proposed product:

Resources and contact people:

Criteria to meet: What are my goals?

Materials I will need and where I might obtain them:

Possible audiences: Inside school: Outside school:

FIGURE 8. PRODUCT PLANNER.

CHAPTER 3

CREATING RUBRICS TO EVALUATE PRODUCTS

Before beginning product development, it is important to establish criteria by which the product will be assessed. From these selected criteria a rubric can be constructed. Begin by listing the components of the proposed product. For example, if the product is a poster, the components might include a title, labels, graphics, and layout. Components will vary according to the expected complexity of the product and the abilities of the student. Students may need to conduct research related to their proposed product in order to determine the components. The rubric starters found in Chapter 4 are a good place to begin. Also, one may consult with an expert in the field to help determine the product components. For example, a cartographer or a geography professor would be an excellent resource for assistance in producing rubric criteria for a map, while an architect would be helpful in determining the features of a blueprint. For ideas on other individuals who might be of assistance, see the community resources listed for each product profiled.

The next step would be to write exemplary characteristics for each component as seen in Figure 9. Students may want to examine good examples of a particular product to determine the exemplary characteristics of each component. It may be helpful for students to find out who is considered to be exemplary producers of this particular product. For example, students might investigate the work of Frank Lloyd Wright for an architectural product or the poetry of Phillis Wheatley if they choose to write a poem.

Once the exemplary characteristics of each component have been listed, performance levels for each characteristic must be set. It is recommended that a four- or six-point scale be used, rather than one that is odd-numbered. With odd-numbered scales there is a tendency for the rater to select the middle value. In addition, if using a numbered scale, each performance level should be defined.

COMPONENT	EXEMPLARY CHARACTERISTICS
POSTER PRODUCT GUIDE	
Title	• Legible, neat • Prominent, visible • Representative of content, appropriate • Correct spelling/grammar
Labels	• Legible, neat • Appropriate placement • Correct spelling/grammar
Graphics	• Clear, visible • Appropriate to theme/content • Add interest, enhance poster
Layout	• Balanced • Noncluttered • Interesting • Emphasis is appropriately placed

FIGURE 9. EXEMPLARY CHARACTERISTICS OF A POSTER.

For example, a "1" may be designated as "Unacceptable" or "Incomplete," and a "4" may signify "Superior" or "Exemplary" production. Figure 10 is an example of a completed rubric that was created using the above procedure. Many ready-made rubrics can be found in books and on the Internet. One Web site that can assist in rubric development is Rubistar (http://rubistar.4teachers.org), which is free to use and supported by the U.S. Department of Education. You can customize the rubrics generated by the site to meet your specific purposes. In addition, resource books related to specific products are helpful in determining the components of, and terminology associated with, particular products.

Teachers can create separate rubrics to evaluate content knowledge and process skills demonstrated during the research and product development phase, or they can incorporate all items related to content, process, and product into one rubric. Other special areas of assessment that may want to be incorporated into a rubric include:

• collaboration with peers,
• creativity, and
• self-evaluation/reflection.

POSTER PRODUCT GUIDE

COMPONENT	EXEMPLARY CHARACTERISTICS	RATINGS
Title	• Legible, neat	1 2 3 4 5 6
	• Prominent, visible	1 2 3 4 5 6
	• Representative of content, appropriate	1 2 3 4 5 6
	• Correct spelling/grammar	1 2 3 4 5 6
Labels	• Legible, neat	1 2 3 4 5 6
	• Appropriate placement	1 2 3 4 5 6
	• Correct spelling/grammar	1 2 3 4 5 6
Graphics	• Clear, visible	1 2 3 4 5 6
	• Appropriate to theme/content	1 2 3 4 5 6
	• Add interest, enhance poster	1 2 3 4 5 6
Layout	• Balanced	1 2 3 4 5 6
	• Noncluttered	1 2 3 4 5 6
	• Interesting	1 2 3 4 5 6
	• Emphasis is appropriately placed	1 2 3 4 5 6

1 = Incomplete
2 = Needs Improvement
3 = Fair
4 = Emerging
5 = Good
6 = Superior

FIGURE 10. SAMPLE RUBRIC FOR A POSTER.

THE ROLE OF STANDARDS

Products developed in the classroom also should have very specific purposes that are closely aligned with curricular goals and state standards. In an age of increased accountability, teachers must ensure that the products students are creating are relevant and address the state's standards and aren't just arbitrary, unconnected tasks. In other words, teachers must think as "assessors" rather than as "activity designers" when assigning products in the classroom. Emphasis should be placed on those performance tasks that will focus instructional work rather than on those projects students just might like to do on a particular topic (Wiggins & McTighe, 2005).

PERFORMANCE-BASED TASKS

When assessing student understanding, it is critical that performance-based tasks are authentic. A project or task is authentic when it (Wiggins & McTighe, 2005):

- simulates the way in which an individual's knowledge is tested in the real world;
- requires students to develop a plan and procedure for solving a problem;
- asks students to simulate the kind of work done by professionals in the field;
- replicates real, complex challenges that adults may face in the workplace;
- requires students to use a repertoire of knowledge and skills to complete complex tasks; and
- allows students the opportunity to practice, obtain feedback, and refine their products and performances.

THE PRODUCTS

The products profiled in this section are listed in alphabetical order. Information for each product is presented in the following format:

....

DEFINITION: Describes the product.

....

TITLE OF THE EXPERT: Job titles of the professionals who create this product.

....

TYPES OF _____: Examples of various types of the product (i.e., for a map, examples might be relief, topographic, globe, etc).

....

WORDS TO KNOW: Terms associated with the product that might be used by professionals creating the product.

....

21ST-CENTURY SKILLS: List of skills that are developed while creating this product.

....

HELPFUL HINTS: Statements of advice professionals might offer to students who create this product.

EXEMPLARY PRODUCERS: Specific individuals who are recognized for expertise in this product.

COMMUNITY RESOURCES: People and places that students might locate within their community to learn more about the product.

BOOKS: Resource books to expand knowledge with regard to this product.

WEB SITES: Internet sites to expand knowledge with regard to this product.

QUOTES TO INSPIRE: Quotes related to the product.

The products profiled in the chapter include:

1. Animation
2. Archive
3. Autobiography
4. Blueprint
5. Commercial
6. Demonstration
7. Documentary
8. Equation
9. Experiment
10. Fairy Tale
11. Family Tree
12. Film
13. Graphic Organizer
14. Handbook
15. Histogram
16. Hologram
17. Illustrated Story
18. Jewelry
19. Journal
20. Logic Puzzle
21. Mask
22. Mosaic
23. Musical Composition
24. Needlecraft
25. Origami
26. Petition
27. Photo Essay
28. Podcast
29. Pop-Up Book
30. Prototype
31. Questionnaire
32. Quilt
33. Recipe
34. Scrapbook
35. Service Project
36. Spreadsheet
37. Terrarium
38. Tessellation
39. Time Capsule
40. Travelogue
41. Video Game
42. WebQuest

PRODUCT: ANIMATION

DEFINITION: A series of drawings, computer graphics, or photographs that give the appearance of motion.

TITLES OF THE EXPERT: Animator, cartoonist

TYPES OF ANIMATION:

- Cel
- Clay
- Computer
- Cut-out
- Flip book
- Puppetoon
- Silhouette
- Stop motion

WORDS TO KNOW:

- Anime
- Aspect ratio
- Breakdowns
- Depth of field
- Dope sheet
- Flash
- Inbetweens
- Key drawings
- Light table
- Maquette
- Optical illusion
- Pinscreen
- Pixel
- Rendering
- Rotoscoping
- Shockwave
- Special effects
- Tweening

21ST-CENTURY SKILLS: Creativity and innovation skills, critical thinking and problem-solving skills, communication skills, collaboration skills, technology skills, media literacy, flexibility and adaptability, initiative and self-direction, social and cross-cultural skills, productivity and accountability, leadership and responsibility, interdisciplinary understanding, mastery of core subjects

HELPFUL HINTS:

- Use a light table when making drawings so they can be layered on top of each other in sequence to refer to when adding or changing another drawing.
- Draw the viewer's attention where you want it by making objects appear or disappear, changing the speed at which an object moves, or adding sound effects.
- Create a strong visual impression by exaggerating or enhancing your images.
- Use your creativity to develop your own original characters.

- Use expressions and the right body language to give your character a distinct personality.
- Keep a sketchbook on hand to record ideas and drawings for future projects.
- Find or create a good workplace that allows you to focus and be creative without distractions.

EXEMPLARY PRODUCERS:

- Art Babbitt
- Joseph Barbera
- Brad Bird
- Mary Blair
- Frank Braxton
- Tim Burton
- Les Clark
- Ron Clements
- Tissa David
- Retta Davidson
- Marc Davis
- Andreas Deja
- Walt Disney
- Lillian Friedman
- William Hanna
- La Verne Harding
- Ollie Johnston
- Milt Kahl
- Glen Keane
- Ward Kimball
- Milton Knight
- John Lasseter
- John Lounsbery
- John Musker
- Floyd Norman
- Joe Ranft
- Wolfgang Reitherman
- Henry Selick
- Retta Scott
- Frank Thomas
- Madilyn Woods
- Marilyn Woods
- Kathy Zielinski

COMMUNITY RESOURCES: Art teacher, journalism teacher, college professors, local animators or cartoonists, technology teacher

BOOKS:

Hahn, D. (1996). *Disney's animation magic: A behind-the-scenes look at how an animated film is made.* New York: Disney Press.

Jenkins, P. (1991). *Animation: How to draw your own flipbooks, and other fun ways to make cartoons move.* Reading, MA: Addison Wesley.

Spilsbury, R. (2008). *Cartoons and animation.* Oxford, England: Heinemann.

WEB SITES:

Cartoonster
http://www.cartoonster.com
Free online tutorial for cartoons and animation.

FluxTime Studio
http://www.fluxtime.com
A free animation community where individuals can create and share animations.

Animation
http://schools.spsd.sk.ca/mountroyal/hoffman/Animation/animindex.html
A wealth of information from tutorials to the history of animation.

QUOTES TO INSPIRE:
"All cartoon characters and fables must be exaggeration, caricatures. It is the very nature of fantasy and fable."—Walt Disney

"The reason to do animation is caricature. Good caricature picks out the essence of the statement and removes everything else. It's not simply about reproducing reality; It's about bumping it up."—Brad Bird

ANIMATION PRODUCT GUIDE	
COMPONENTS	EXEMPLARY CHARACTERISTICS
Appearance	• Images are of high quality • Color balance/choices enhance the overall presentation
Motion	• Effectively uses path layering to show direction for the animation to follow • Effectively and frequently uses motion tweening • Effectively and frequently uses shape tweening • Smooth and fluid transitions
Project Management	• Each group member contributed equally • Projected deadlines were met
Sound/Music	• Adds to the overall quality • Synchronized, well timed with the overall animation • Uses multiple audio effects or layers
Storyboard	• Fully developed, considers all elements of project • Fluid and cohesive, follows logical sequence
Title and Credits	• Attractively presented • Easy to read • Appropriate style/design for content • All permissions to use content/graphics "borrowed" from Web pages or scanned from other publications have been secured

PRODUCT: ARCHIVE

DEFINITION: A compilation of firsthand facts, data, and evidence brought together for a specific reason.

TITLES OF THE EXPERT: Archivist, curator, librarian, preservationist

TYPES OF ARCHIVES:
- Audio
- Electronic
- Experiential
- Living
- Paper
- Visual

WORDS TO KNOW:
- Aberrant date
- Accession
- Acquisition
- Appraisal
- Authority control
- Classification
- Collection
- Copyright
- Dark archives
- Deed of gift
- Description
- Disposal
- Finding aid
- Fonds
- Forgery
- Inventory
- Light archives
- Manuscript
- Provenance
- Record group
- Repository

21ST-CENTURY SKILLS: Civic literacy, creativity and innovation skills, critical thinking and problem-solving skills, communication skills, collaboration skills, information literacy, technology skills, media literacy, flexibility and adaptability, initiative and self-direction, social and cross-cultural skills, productivity and accountability, leadership and responsibility, interdisciplinary understanding, mastery of core subjects

HELPFUL HINTS:
- Evaluate the collection and decide if the contents are important enough to preserve.
- Organize into smaller categories. For instance, a family photo collection might be organized by year, family member, or special occasion.
- Create a finding aid as a guide to help others locate items in the collection.
- Store important papers under conditions that are similar to what most people find comfortable for themselves. Never store paper documents

in areas of high heat and moisture. High heat causes paper to become brittle and discolored, and too much moisture allows destructive mold to grow. Light also is a serious danger to paper documents, especially fluorescent and natural light. It causes the paper to break down chemically and fades the ink.

- Store papers in appropriately sized containers that will protect them from physical damage and dust.

EXEMPLARY PRODUCERS:

- Otto Bettmann
- Paul Castiglia
- Elena S. Danielson
- Bob DeFlores
- Johan Feith
- Robert Fruin
- Sir Hilary Jenkinson
- Lao-Tzu
- Michael Lampen
- Alan Lomax
- Samuel Muller
- Margaret Cross Norton
- Ernst Posner
- T. R. Schellenberg
- John Taylor
- Adrienne Thomas

COMMUNITY RESOURCES: College professors, local archivists, librarians, museum curators

BOOKS:

Block, I. (Ed.). (2000). *Saving America's treasures.* Washington, DC: National Geographic Society.

Ritzenthaler, M. L. (1993). *Preserving archives and manuscripts.* Chicago: Society of American Archivists.

Sturdevant, K. S. (2002). *Organizing & preserving your heirloom documents.* Cincinnati, OH: Betterway Books.

WEB SITES:

The National Archives
http://www.archives.gov
Information on the archives of the U.S. Federal government and other American historical documents.

The Society of American Archivists
http://www.archivists.org
North America's oldest and largest national archival professional association.

QUOTES TO INSPIRE:
"The constant dilemma of the information age is that our ability to gather a sea of data greatly exceeds the tools and techniques available to sort, extract, and apply the information we've collected."—Jeff Davidson

"There is no knowledge, no light, no wisdom that you are in possession of, but what you have received it from some source."—Brigham Young

ARCHIVE PRODUCT GUIDE	
COMPONENTS	EXEMPLARY CHARACTERISTICS
Arrangement/Organization	• Arranged/organized by provenance and/or original order
Description/Documentation	• Appropriate and accurate documentation accompanies each medium included within the archive
Media (e.g., documents, letters, photographs, video, sound recordings)	• Appropriately selected for their enduring value and historical context
Preservation	• Stored to ensure long-term preservation

PRODUCT: AUTOBIOGRAPHY

DEFINITION: An account of a person's life written by that person.

TITLES OF THE EXPERT: Author, writer

TYPES OF AUTOBIOGRAPHIES:

- Celebrity
- Epiphany
- Fantasy/Fictional
- Memoir
- Reflective
- Sensationalist
- Traditional/ Personal essay

WORDS TO KNOW:

- Biography
- Dedication
- Foreword
- Genealogy
- Ghostwriter
- Memorabilia
- Narrative

21ST-CENTURY SKILLS: Communication skills, technology skills, initiative and self-direction, productivity and accountability, mastery of core subjects

HELPFUL HINTS:

- Read some good autobiographies before writing your own to get a feel for how to organize and structure yours.
- Develop a theme that drives your story and makes it compelling. Think about what has been most important to you in your life and focus your story around it.
- Decide how to organize your autobiography. Chronological order naturally is the most popular method, but you can decide whether to start the story before you were born, at your birth, or sometime later.
- Refresh your memory by finding things from your past that remind you of different events in your past. Old photographs, letters, and memorabilia can spark memories to include in your story.
- Edit your work for correct grammar, spelling, and readability.

Exemplary Producers:

- Maya Angelou
- Fidel Castro
- Charles Darwin
- Frederick Douglass
- Anne Frank
- Ben Franklin
- Ulysses S. Grant
- Thomas Jefferson
- Helen Keller
- Barack Obama
- Ronald Reagan
- Mark Twain
- Malcolm X

Community Resources: Family members, friends, former teachers, English teacher

Book:

Fletcher, R. J. (2007). *How to write your life story.* New York: Collins.

Web Site:

BrainPop Jr.—Writing About Yourself
http://www.brainpopjr.com/writing/nonfiction/writingaboutyourself/preview.weml
Animated, curriculum-based content that engages students in autobiography.

Quotes to Inspire:

"One of the most attractive things about writing your autobiography is that you're not dead."—Joseph Barbera

"Autobiography is only to be trusted when it reveals something disgraceful. A man who gives a good account of himself is probably lying, since any life when viewed from the inside is simply a series of defeats."—George Orwell

AUTOBIOGRAPHY PRODUCT GUIDE	
COMPONENTS	**EXEMPLARY CHARACTERISTICS**
Conclusion	• Strong • Leaves the reader satisfied
Content	• Full of quality details and elaboration, reader gets a true sense of who the writer is • Goes beyond the obvious or predictable
Dialogue (Optional)	• Highly detailed, insightful, and thoughtful • Enhances the reader's understanding of the writer
Introduction	• Inviting • Previews the structure of the work
Mechanics	• Appropriate use of grammar • Free of spelling errors • Strong evidence of proofreading
Sequence/ Organization	• Presented in a logical order • Effectively keeps the interest of the reader

PRODUCT: BLUEPRINT

DEFINITION: A type of paper-based reproduction, usually of a technical drawing, documenting an architectural or an engineering design.

TITLES OF THE EXPERT: Architect, designer, draftsperson, planner, engineer, builder

TYPES OF BLUEPRINTS:

- Carpentry
- Electrical
- Mechanical
- Plumbing
- Ship
- Sheet metal
- Structural
- Welding

WORDS TO KNOW:

- Application block
- Architecture
- Bill of material block
- Computer-aided design
- Construction
- Digital displays
- Drawing number
- Finish marks
- Floor plan
- Information blocks
- Offset printing
- Reference number
- Revision block
- Scale
- Scale block
- Technical drawing
- Title block
- Whiteprint
- Zone number

21ST-CENTURY SKILLS: Financial, economic, and/or business literacy; entrepreneurial literacy; civic literacy; creativity and innovation skills; critical thinking and problem-solving skills; communication skills; collaboration skills; technology skills; media literacy; flexibility and adaptability; initiative and self-direction; productivity and accountability; leadership and responsibility; interdisciplinary understanding; mastery of core subjects

HELPFUL HINTS:

- Design a scale drawing of what you want to build on graph paper.
- Decide on symbols to use that represent doors, windows, etc. on your scale drawing.
- Record scale size on your diagram.

Exemplary Producers:

- Leonardo da Vinci
- Buckminster Fuller
- Wenzel Hollar
- Julia Morgan
- Gyo Obata
- I. M. Pei
- Aleksandr Rodchenko
- Frank Lloyd Wright

Community Resources: Drafting teacher, local architect, college professors

Books:

Glenn, P. B. (1993). *Under every roof: A kid's style and field guide to the architecture of American houses.* Washington, DC: Preservation Press, National Trust for Historic Preservation.

Thorne-Thomsen, K. (1994). *Frank Lloyd Wright for kids.* Chicago: Chicago Review Press.

Web Sites:

Archkidecture
http://www.archkidecture.org
An independent architecture education project that encourages children to explore and participate in the built environment.

Architect Studio 3D
http://architectstudio3d.org/AS3d/home.html
Design a house online with the Frank Lloyd Wright Preservation Trust.

Quotes to Inspire:

"I know the price of success: dedication, hard work and an unremitting devotion to the things you want to see happen."—Frank Lloyd Wright

"I think my best skill as an architect is the achievement of hand-to-eye coordination. I am able to transfer a sketch into a model into the building."—Frank Gehry

BLUEPRINT PRODUCT GUIDE	
COMPONENTS	EXEMPLARY CHARACTERISTICS
Appearance	• Professional in quality • Lines are clean, neat, and straight (where appropriate) • All essential elements are included • Logical, accurately depicts the desired view
Legend/Key	• Neat • Easy to find/read • Employs use of standard symbols where appropriate • All symbols are identified and their meaning clearly denoted
Scale	• Appropriately drawn to scale, accurate measurements/proportions • Easy to interpret • Identified/indicated on plan
Titles/Labels	• Neat • Prominent where appropriate • Appropriately placed • Correct spelling/grammar

PRODUCT: COMMERCIAL

DEFINITION: An advertisement on television or radio.

TITLES OF THE EXPERT: Commercial director, commercial writer

TYPES OF COMMERCIALS:
- Associated user imagery
- Bandwagon
- Benefit/Cause
- Comparison
- Demonstration
- Emotional words
- Exemplary story
- Ongoing characters or celebrities
- Parody or borrowed format
- Present the need or problem
- Repeated words
- Symbol, analogy, or exaggerated graphic (illustrating the benefit)
- Symbol, analogy, or exaggerated graphic (representing the problem)
- Testimonial
- Transfer
- Unique personality property

WORDS TO KNOW:
- Concept
- Copywriter
- Jingle
- Logo
- Market
- Media
- Persuasion
- Promotion
- Shoot
- Slogan
- Storyboard
- Target audience
- Voiceover

21ST-CENTURY SKILLS:
Global awareness; financial, economic, and/or business literacy; entrepreneurial literacy; civic literacy; creativity and innovation skills; critical thinking and problem-solving skills; communication skills; collaboration skills; information literacy; technology skills; media literacy; flexibility and adaptability; initiative and self-direction; social and cross-cultural skills; productivity and accountability; leadership and responsibility; interdisciplinary understanding; mastery of core subjects

HELPFUL HINTS:
- Keep your audience in mind during all phases of development.
- Prepare ahead of time and write down what you want to say.
- Practice until the script becomes second nature.

- Wear solid colors, not busy patterns or stripes, as these can distract from your message.
- Design a logo and a slogan for your product or service.
- Use creative and attention-getting methods for introducing your product or service.
- Find a place with good lighting to film the commercial.
- Think visually. Show and tell.
- Keep it short and to the point. Most commercials are 30 seconds in length.
- Ensure that copyrighted images and music are not used illegally.
- Make sure the audio and video match.
- End the commercial with the "call for action" or the main message that you want others to receive regarding the product or service.
- Keep your message consistent so the audience becomes familiar with your product or service.

Exemplary Producers:

- Fredrik Bond
- Bryan Buckley
- Frank Budgen
- Tom Carty
- Stuart Douglas
- Jonathan Glazer
- Daniel Kleinman
- Pontus Lowenhielm
- Chris Palmer
- Ivan Zacharias

Community Resources: Marketing experts, local directors, business owners

Book:

Graydon, S., & Clark, W. (2003). *Made you look: How advertising works and why you should know.* Toronto: Annick Press.

Web Sites:

PBS Kids Don't Buy It: Get Media Smart

http://pbskids.org/dontbuyit/advertisingtricks

A media literacy Web site for young people that encourages users to think critically about media and become smart consumers.

Kids' Vid

http://kidsvid.altec.org

An instructional Web site to help students and teachers use video production in the classroom.

Quotes to Inspire:

"You have only 30 seconds in a TV commercial. If you grab attention in the first frame with a visual surprise, you stand a better chance of holding the viewer. People screen out a lot of commercials because they open with something dull . . . When you advertise fire-extinguishers, open with the fire."—David Ogilvy

"In general, my children refuse to eat anything that hasn't danced on television."—Erma Bombeck

COMMERCIAL PRODUCT GUIDE

Components	Exemplary Characteristics
Dialogue/ Narration	• Main message is clearly expressed • Supported by images and setting • Selected with attention to persuasive appeal • Shows confidence, conviction, and enthusiasm
Duration	• Presented within established timeframe
Message/ Content	• Clear and focused • Appropriate to audience • Includes a propaganda/persuasive technique
Music	• Elicits a rich emotional response • Supports and/or enhances message/story
Organization/ Planning	• Well-rehearsed • Effective continuity/flow • Dynamic, holds audience attention
Persuasiveness/ Propaganda Techniques	• Presents strong arguments/reasons • Elaborates appropriately • Anticipates and addresses possible audience concerns • Embeds prior knowledge, personal experience, and/or reflection into the argument
Props and Costumes	• Enhance message • Selected in consideration of copyright issues
Storyboard	• Detailed and complete • Effectively incorporates text with images/sketches • Reflects thorough planning • Presented in a manner that effectively organizes all aspects of the project (transitions, special effects, sound, etc.)
Technical Aspects (Video and Audio)	• Effective camera use: Video is of high quality, images are crisp and sharp at all times, smooth transitions • Effective audio/sound: Corresponds with images, crisp and smooth, free of ambient/background noise

PRODUCT: DEMONSTRATION

DEFINITION: A method of teaching by example or showing rather than verbally explaining.

....

TITLES OF THE EXPERT: Speaker, lecturer

....

TYPES OF DEMONSTRATIONS:

- Computer
- Exhibits
- Oral
- Performances
- Posters
- Workshop

....

WORDS TO KNOW:

- Adaptation
- Attention span
- Body language
- Conclusion
- Diagram
- Eye contact
- Gestures
- Information overload
- Introduction
- Organization
- Preparation
- Rehearse
- Stage fright
- Structure
- Style
- Visual aid

....

21ST-CENTURY SKILLS: Creativity and innovation skills, critical thinking and problem-solving skills, communication skills, collaboration skills, information literacy, technology skills, media literacy, flexibility and adaptability, initiative and self-direction, social and cross-cultural skills, productivity and account-ability, leadership and responsibility, interdisciplinary understanding, mastery of core subjects

....

HELPFUL HINTS:

- Select a topic or idea that can be shown and told in the time allowed.
- Outline the key points you want to make and how each might be demonstrated.
- Determine the equipment that will be needed.
- Practice in front of a mirror or in front of your parents to ensure fluidity.
- Speak clearly and use appropriate grammar.
- Maintain good posture.
- Make sure you have all of your materials together and they are easily accessible before beginning.

- Make sure all audience members can see what you are doing.
- Watch the faces of the people in the audience. If their faces show that they do not understand you may need to repeat a point.

EXEMPLARY PRODUCERS:

- Cat Cora
- George Foreman
- John King
- Emeril Lagasse
- Bill Nye

- Rachael Ray
- Martha Stewart
- Scott "Carrot Top" Thompson
- Bob Villa

COMMUNITY RESOURCES: Speech teacher, college professors, community speaker

BOOKS:

Raymer, D. (2005). *School smarts projects: Create tons of great presentations, boost your creativity, improve your grades, and save time and trouble!* Middleton, WI: American Girl.

Somervill, B. A. (2007). *What did you find out?: Reporting conclusions.* New York: PowerKids Press.

WEB SITES:

Allyn & Bacon Public Speaking Web Site
http://wps.ablongman.com/ab_public_speaking_2
Modules to learn more about the process of public speaking.

Discovery Education—Science Fair Central
http://school.discoveryeducation.com/sciencefaircentral
Useful tools and resources for science fair planning, including presentations.

QUOTES TO INSPIRE:

"The problem with communication . . . is the *illusion* that it has been accomplished."—George Bernard Shaw

"There are two types of speakers: those that are nervous and those that are liars."—Mark Twain

DEMONSTRATION PRODUCT GUIDE

Components	Exemplary Characteristics
Performance/Presentation	• Engaging, captures audience attention • Precise in technique • Demonstrates confidence and enthusiasm
Preparation	• All materials are in working order and readily accessible • Evidence of prior rehearsal
Props	• Add interest or clarity, not distracting
Script	• Accurate and precise • Highlights key concepts • Enhances demonstration
Suitability	• Effectively demonstrates concept
Visibility	• Suitably sized equipment/props/materials • Background enhances visibility/not distracting • Sufficient lighting • Appropriate elevation to ensure all audience members have clear view

PRODUCT: DOCUMENTARY

DEFINITION: A nonfiction film that depicts some aspect of reality.

TITLES OF THE EXPERT: Documentary filmmaker, director

TYPES OF DOCUMENTARIES:

- Compilation
- Ethnographic
- Expository
- Interactive
- Mondo film
- Narrative
- Observational
- Participatory mode
- Performative mode
- Poetic mode
- Raw footage
- Reflective

WORDS TO KNOW:

- Cinema vérité
- Commentary
- Conflict of interest
- Direct cinema
- Editing
- Framing
- Intertitle
- Long take
- Narration
- Objectivity
- Perspective
- Point of view
- Profilmic event
- Realism
- Voice of authority
- Voiceover

21ST-CENTURY SKILLS:
Global awareness, civic literacy, creativity and innovation skills, critical thinking and problem-solving skills, communication skills, collaboration skills, information literacy, technology skills, media literacy, flexibility and adaptability, initiative and self-direction, social and cross-cultural skills, productivity and accountability, leadership and responsibility, interdisciplinary understanding, mastery of core subjects

HELPFUL HINTS:

- Choose a topic that is compelling and that a variety of people can relate to.
- Use index cards to organize elements of the film into the order that works best.
- Incorporate other media such as newspaper clippings and old photographs.

EXEMPLARY PRODUCERS:

- Michael Apted
- Orlando Bagwell
- Ken Burns
- Laurent Cantet
- Roger Donaldson
- Alex Gibney
- Al Gore
- Chris Hegedus
- Ted Leonsis
- Michael Moore
- Errol Morris
- Kimberly Peirce
- Terry Sanders
- Martin Scorsese

COMMUNITY RESOURCES: Journalists, professors of film studies

BOOKS:

Hampe, B. (2007). *Making documentary films and videos: A practical guide to planning, filming, and editing documentaries.* New York: Holt.

Wormser, R. (2002). *To the young filmmaker: Conversations with working film-makers.* New York: Franklin Watts.

WEB SITES:

Documentary Filmmaking for Teens
http://understandmedia.com/art030.htm
Learn how to make documentary films.

Documenting the Face of America
http://www.documentingamerica.org
A film that tells the stories of photographers whose assignments were to document Americans living and struggling in the time of the Great Depression.

QUOTES TO INSPIRE:

"If it can be written, or thought, it can be filmed."—Stanley Kubrick

"Photography is a way of feeling, of touching, of loving. What you have caught on film is captured forever . . . it remembers little things, long after you have forgotten everything."—Aaron Siskind

DOCUMENTARY PRODUCT GUIDE

Components	Exemplary Characteristics
Audio	• Corresponds with images • Crisp and smooth • Free of ambient/background noise
Camera Work/Effects	• Steady and captures all important images • Appropriate and carefully planned camera positions, camera angles, and zooms • Effective use of visual effects that add interest and enhance the message, not overstated
Dialogue/Narration	• Clearly audible • Complements images
Lighting	• All images, important scenery, and props are clearly visible at all appropriate times • Appropriate modifications to the lighting have been made to enhance the presentation
Music	• Appropriate to content, sets desired mood/tone • Complements and enhances subject matter • Appropriate use of tempos and volume levels to highlight important scenes and/or dialogue
Organization	• Clearly and logically sequenced • Effectively guides the viewer through topic
Quality of Information/Accuracy	• Essential information presented and supported with relevant details and/or examples • Assertions are fully supported • All information is accurate
Script	• Thoughtfully scripted in order to create an organized, focused presentation of information • Of professional quality
Transitions	• Smooth and thoughtful, effectively moves from one part to the next • Clearly show how ideas are connected
Video	• High quality • Crisp and sharp at all times • Moves smoothly from shot to shot, seamless

PRODUCT: EQUATION

DEFINITION: An arithmetic expression that equates one set of conditions to another; for example, $A + B = C$.

TITLE OF THE EXPERT: Mathematician

TYPES OF EQUATIONS:

- Absolute value(s)
- Algebraic
- Binomial
- Cubic
- Elliptic
- Exponential
- Fractions
- Functional
- Hyperbolic
- Integral
- Linear
- Logarithmic
- Ordinary differential
- Parabolic
- Partial differential
- Quadratic
- Radicals
- Reciprocal
- Trigonometric

WORDS TO KNOW:

- Coefficient
- Constants
- Derivative
- Expressions
- Isolating
- Sequences
- Root
- Simplifying
- Variables

21ST-CENTURY SKILLS: Creativity and innovation skills, critical thinking and problem-solving skills, communication skills, flexibility and adaptability, initiative and self-direction, mastery of core subjects

HELPFUL HINTS:

- First identify what unknown quantity you are trying to find, because this variable is the value that you will be solving for. Give this unknown quantity a letter name such as x.
- Look at the rest of the information you do have. Think about what you are solving for, and only use the information that helps you find it.
- Look for key words to determine mathematical operations.
- Decide how the values you have relate to one another.
- Write the equation so that the variable, x, is equal to the values that you know and their relationships to each other and the variable.

- Whatever you do to an equation, make sure you do the same thing to both sides.
- Always check your work to ensure accuracy.

....

Exemplary Producers:

- Maria Gaetana Agnesi
- Olusola Akinyele
- Archimedes
- Āryabhaṭa
- Charles Babbage
- Jacob Bernoulli
- Friedrich Bessel
- Gertrude Blanch
- Gerolamo Cardano
- Mary Cartwright
- Augustin Louis Cauchy
- Ernesto Cesàro
- Ethelbert Chukwu
- Maria Cinquini-Cibrario
- Albert Einstein
- Jean Baptiste Joseph Fourier
- Erik Ivar Fredholm
- Carl Friedrich Gauss
- David Hilbert
- Carl Gustav Jacob Jacobi
- Olga Alexandrovna Ladyzhenskaya
- Pierre-Simon Laplace
- Andrei Andreyevich Markov
- Sir Isaac Newton
- Amalie Emmy Noether
- Blaise Pascal
- Carle David Tolm Runge
- George Gabriel Stokes
- Sharaf al-Dīn al-Ṭūsī
- François Viète
- Floyd Williams

....

Community Resources: Math teacher, college professors

....

Book:

Bruno, L. C., & Baker, L. W. (1999). *Math and mathematicians: The history of math discoveries around the world*. Detroit, MI: U-X-L.

....

Web Sites:

Math Central

http://mathcentral.uregina.ca/index.php
A site for math students and teachers that offers resources and answers to math questions.

Purplemath

http://www.purplemath.com
Helps students gain understanding and self-confidence in algebra.

EqWorld—Mathematical World of Equations

http://eqworld.ipmnet.ru

Presents extensive information on solutions to various classes of ordinary differential, partial differential, integral, functional, and other mathematical equations.

....

QUOTES TO INSPIRE:

"We could use up two eternities in learning all that is to be learned about our own world and the thousands of nations that have arisen and flourished and vanished from it. Mathematics alone would occupy me eight million years."— Mark Twain

"Can you do Division? Divide a loaf by a knife—what's the answer to *that*?"— Lewis Carroll

EQUATION PRODUCT GUIDE	
COMPONENTS	EXEMPLARY CHARACTERISTICS
Communication/ Explanation	• Accurately and effectively describes the relationship represented in the equation • Uses appropriate terminology/vocabulary associated with the discipline • Effectively communicates reasoning process
Computation	• Correctly completes and solves the equation, free of mathematical error
Process	• Effectively and accurately translates idea/ situation into an equation • Shows all operations that lead to an appropriate solution
Verification	• Thoroughly checks computation and relationship for accuracy

PRODUCT: EXPERIMENT

DEFINITION: A test under controlled conditions that is made to demonstrate a known truth, examine the validity of a hypothesis, or determine the usefulness of something previously untried.

TITLE OF THE EXPERT: Scientist

TYPES OF EXPERIMENTS:
- Controlled
- External links
- Field studies
- Laboratory
- Natural
- Observational studies
- Qualitative
- Quantitative
- Quasi
- Single subject
- True

WORDS TO KNOW:
- Controlled variable
- Correlation
- Data
- Dependent variable
- Effect
- Factor
- Findings
- Hypothesis
- Independent variable
- Measure
- Methodology
- Objective
- Observation
- Prediction
- Randomization
- Reliability
- Replication
- Scientific method
- Stimulus
- Subject
- Treatment group
- Validity

21ST-CENTURY SKILLS: Critical thinking and problem-solving skills, communication skills, collaboration skills, information literacy, technology skills, initiative and self-direction, productivity and accountability, mastery of core subjects

HELPFUL HINTS:
- Think about what you are interested in and develop a question that can be tested.
- Be specific about the problem you will investigate.
- Write a hypothesis, or prediction, of what you expect the results will be of your experiment.
- Make sure your experiment can be carried out with the materials you have available or materials that can be obtained easily.

- Keep good records of everything you do related to your experiment, even the mistakes.
- Repeat your experiment several times to make sure you get the same results each time.
- Think about documenting your experiment from the beginning with photographs and/or scientific illustrations.
- Use tables and graphs to organize and display the data generated from your experiment.
- Remember that an experiment is not a failure if it proves your hypothesis wrong.
- Always wear safety goggles whenever you are working with chemicals or other substances that might get into your eyes.
- Wash your hands before and after each experiment.

EXEMPLARY PRODUCERS:

- Alexander Graham Bell
- Rachel Carson
- George Washington Carver
- Marie Curie
- Thomas Edison
- Albert Einstein
- Michael Faraday
- Benjamin Franklin
- Galileo Galilei
- Fabiola Gianotti
- Jane Goodall
- Heinrich Hertz
- David Hume
- Sir Isaac Newton
- Guglielmo Marconi
- Gregor Mendel
- Stanley Milgram
- Robert Millikan
- Samuel Morse
- Louis Pasteur
- Linus Pauling
- Ivan Pavlov
- Anita Roberts
- B. F. Skinner
- Orville and Wilbur Wright

COMMUNITY RESOURCES: Science teachers, college professors, inventors

BOOKS:

Somervill, B. A. (2007). *What do you want to prove?: Planning investigations.* New York: PowerKids Press.

The Exploratorium. (2006). *Exploratopia: More than 400 kid-friendly experiments and explorations for curious minds.* New York: Little, Brown.

WEB SITES:

Bill Nye the Science Guy
http://www.billnye.com
View episode guides and demos of Bill Nye's science show online.

ZoomSci
http://pbskids.org/zoom/activities/sci
Lists instructions for many science experiments shown on the PBS television show, *Zoom.*

....

QUOTES TO INSPIRE:
"I love fools' experiments. I am always making them."—Charles Darwin

"I am told that there have been over the years a number of experiments taking place in places like Massachusetts Institute of Technology that have been entirely based on concepts raised by *Star Trek.*"—Patrick Stewart

EXPERIMENT PRODUCT GUIDE	
COMPONENTS	EXEMPLARY CHARACTERISTICS
Data	• Carefully collected with appropriate precision • Accurately represented in tables and/or graphs
Experimental Design	• Effectively tests the hypothesis • Relevant, demonstrates that the problem has been thoroughly analyzed • All variables appropriately identified
Hypothesis	• Thoroughly developed • Clearly identified and stated
Procedures	• Clear and logically sequenced • Completion of all steps as planned in the experiment • Abides by all safety regulations
Results/Conclusions	• Clearly presented • Easily interpreted • Directly address hypothesis • Sound and supported by the data
Title	• Reflective of the experiment, gives insight into what the experiment is about

PRODUCT: FAIRY TALE

DEFINITION: A fictional story, usually for children, that may feature folkloric characters (such as fairies or talking animals) and enchantments, and often involves a far-fetched sequence of events.

TITLES OF THE EXPERT: Author, writer, storyteller, librarian

TYPES OF FAIRY TALES:
- Contemporary
- Fractured
- Literary
- Traditional

WORDS TO KNOW:
- Enchantment
- Fantasy
- Folklore
- Genre Hero/ Heroine
- Magic
- Moral
- Protagonist

21ST-CENTURY SKILLS: Global awareness, creativity and innovation skills, critical thinking and problem-solving skills, communication skills, technology skills, initiative and self-direction, productivity and accountability, mastery of core subjects

HELPFUL HINTS:
- Fairy tales usually are morality stories, so choose a moral for your fairy tale before you start to write.
- Create a good main character that your audience will like and want to have a happy ending.
- You also will need to create an evil character to cause trouble for your good character. The evil character usually has magical powers of some sort and uses them to harm the good characters in the story.
- Think up a magical element for your tale, whether it is a character or an object. You should have both good and evil magical forces to balance one another in the story.
- Decide what challenges your good character will have to overcome in the story. They should seem almost impossible to win and should require some creative thinking by your hero and usually a bit of magical help.

- Wrap up your story with a "happily ever after" ending. Your good character should emerge victorious and the bad guy should be soundly defeated.

EXEMPLARY PRODUCERS:

- Aesop
- Hans Christian Andersen
- Lyman Frank Baum
- Ashley Bryan
- Lewis Carroll
- Charles Dickens
- Jacob Ludwig Grimm
- Wilhelm Carl Grimm
- Joel Chandler Harris
- Tanith Lee
- Jeanne-Marie Leprince de Beaumont
- Gail Carson Levine
- Robin McKinley
- Charles Perrault
- Jon Scieszka
- Mark Twain
- Oscar Wilde
- Terri Windling
- Jane Yolen

COMMUNITY RESOURCES: English/Creative writing teacher, college professor, librarian, local authors

BOOKS:

Rosinsky, N. M. (2009). *Write your own fable*. Minneapolis, MN: Capstone.
Warren, C. (2008). *How to write stories*. Laguna Hills, CA: QEB.

WEB SITES:

Scholastic's Myths, Folktales, and Fairy Tales

http://teacher.scholastic.com/writewit/mff
Students can study and create original work in each of these important literary genres.

ReadWriteThink—Fractured Fairy Tales

http://www.readwritethink.org/materials/fairytales
Interactive tool used to compose a fractured fairy tale.

QUOTES TO INSPIRE:

"Some day you will be old enough to start reading fairy tales again."—C. S. Lewis

"Fairy tales are more than true; not because they tell us that dragons exist, but because they tell us that dragons can be beaten."—G. K. Chesterton

FAIRY TALE PRODUCT GUIDE	
COMPONENTS	EXEMPLARY CHARACTERISTICS
Characters	• Vividly described (appearance and action) • Complex • Interesting
Conflict/Problem	• Well developed • Interesting/engaging, sparks interests • Convincing, logical • Satisfying resolution
Dialogue/Narration	• Effectively conveys mood • Incorporates rich language
Illustrations (optional)	• Enhance story
Mechanics	• Appropriate use of grammar • Free of spelling errors • Strong evidence of proofreading
Organization	• Logical sequence of events • Engaging beginning • Satisfying conclusion • Clear transitions • Fluid and coherent
Setting	• Vivid, descriptive • Enhances story • Conveys time, location, weather
Theme/Moral/Lesson	• Clearly conveyed by end of story
Vocabulary	• Vivid, precise, and sophisticated

PRODUCT: FAMILY TREE

DEFINITION: A graphical representation of how family members are related.

TITLES OF THE EXPERT: Genealogist, historian, archivist, librarian

TYPES OF FAMILY TREES:

- Ahnentafel chart
- Ancestor chart
- Digital
- Genogram
- Pedigree chart
- Photo montage
- Text

WORDS TO KNOW:

- Ancestor
- Bequest
- Birth records
- Cadastra
- Census data
- Codicil
- Collateral ancestor
- Consanguinity
- Death records
- Deed
- Domesday Book
- Dowry
- Emigration
- Enumeration
- Estate
- Executor
- GEDCOM
- Grantee
- Grantor
- Heirloom
- Heraldry
- Immigration records
- Intestate
- Land deeds
- Lineage
- Nuclear family
- Patronymics
- Posthumous
- Primogenitor
- Probate
- Progeny
- Relictus
- Sine prole
- Soundex
- Surname
- Testate
- Vital records
- Wills

21ST-CENTURY SKILLS: Global awareness, civic literacy, creativity and innovation skills, critical thinking and problem-solving skills, communication skills, collaboration skills, information literacy, technology skills, initiative and self-direction, social and cross-cultural skills, productivity and accountability, interdisciplinary understanding, mastery of core subjects

HELPFUL HINTS:

- Start by writing down what you already know about the people in your family.
- Ask your relatives about other family members because this will save time and effort searching for records.

- Use credible sources.
- Locate and review original records when possible.
- Make sure that all of your documents are well organized so you can evaluate them more easily when creating your family tree.
- Store information using notebooks, index cards, and files or by using computer software or an online service.

....

Exemplary Producers:

- Arthur Adams
- Anthony Adolph
- Elizabeth Petty Bentley
- John Insley Coddington
- Meredith B. Colket, Jr.
- William Wyman Fiske
- Alex Haley

- Cyndi Howells
- Marcela Moreno
- John O'Hart
- Josef Pilnacek
- Bryan Sykes
- Stephen Thomas

....

Community Resources: Librarian, local genealogical society, local historical association

....

Books:

Beller, S. P. (2007). *Roots for kids: A genealogy guide for young people* (2nd ed.). Baltimore: Genealogical Publishing Company.

Shepherdson, N. (2003). *Ancestor hunt: Finding your family online.* New York: Children's Press.

Wolfman, I. (2002). *Climbing your family tree: Online and offline genealogy for kids.* New York: Workman.

....

Web Sites:

PBS—Grow a Tree
http://pbskids.org/wayback/family/tree
Interactive tool that allows students to create their own family tree.

USGenWeb Kidz
http://www.rootsweb.ancestry.com/~usgwkidz
The children's version of this popular genealogy Web site.

QUOTES TO INSPIRE:

"Genealogy, n. An account of one's descent from a man who did not particularly care to trace his own."—Ambrose Bierce

"In all of us there is a hunger, marrow-deep, to know our heritage—to know who we are and where we have come from. Without this enriching knowledge, there is a hollow yearning. No matter what our attainments in life, there is still a vacuum. An emptiness. And the most disquieting loneliness."—Alex Haley

FAMILY TREE PRODUCT GUIDE	
COMPONENTS	EXEMPLARY CHARACTERISTICS
Appearance/Layout	• Visually pleasing, attractive • Easy to read • Appropriate to content
Data and Information	• Proper pedigree lines • At least four generations presented • Accurate • Organized in a way that is visually effective • Sufficient and relevant resources were consulted to gather information (i.e., birth, marriage, and death records; family Bibles; deeds; letters; journals; old photographs; wills; and naturalization papers)
Photographs/Images	• Enhance content • Correspond to labels/text • Visually appealing
Relationship Labels	• Appropriately placed • Neat and legible • Correctly identified • Incorporate important dates, relationships, and other vital information

PRODUCT: FILM

DEFINITION: A form of entertainment that enacts a story by sound and a sequence of images, giving the illusion of continuous movement.

TITLE OF THE EXPERT: Film director

TYPES OF FILM:

- Amateur
- Animated
- Anthology
- Art
- Avant-garde
- Biographical
- Blockbusters
- Cult
- Dance
- Documentary
- Dramas
- Ecology
- Experimental
- Exploration
- Independent
- Low budget
- Narrative
- Nonfiction
- Propaganda
- Short
- Travel

WORDS TO KNOW:

- Aperture
- Aspect ratio
- Blue screen
- Casting
- Cinematography
- Clapperboard
- Craning
- Cutaway
- Dailies
- Director's cut
- Depth of field
- Dollying
- Field of view
- Film stock
- Final cut
- Foley
- Frame
- Gaffer
- Montage
- Panning
- Perspective
- Production
- Projection
- Rough cut
- Scores
- Screening
- Script
- Set
- Sound stage
- Splicing
- Storyboard
- Stuntman
- Tracking
- Zoetrope

21ST-CENTURY SKILLS: Creativity and innovation skills, critical thinking and problem-solving skills, communication skills, collaboration skills, information literacy, technology skills, media literacy, flexibility and adaptability, initiative and self-direction, social and cross-cultural skills, productivity and accountability, leadership and responsibility, interdisciplinary understanding, mastery of core subjects

....

Helpful Hints:
- If you are having trouble thinking of an introduction, imagine the end first, and start the movie there.
- Secure required permissions if using copyrighted material.
- Use different types of shots (close-up, far away, etc.) to add visual interest.
- Make sure the actors can be heard and understood and that ambient/background noises are not distracting.
- Prepare the video camera in advance by making sure the battery is fully charged. If possible, have a spare battery on hand to increase filming time.
- Be sure to add credits at the end to acknowledge all contributions.

....

Exemplary Producers:
- Woody Allen
- Robert Altman
- Ingmar Bergman
- Danny Boyle
- James Cameron
- Jane Campion
- Charlie Chaplin
- Shirley Clarke
- Francis Ford Coppola
- Sofia Coppola
- Lee Daniels
- Julie Dash
- Cheryl Dunye
- Clint Eastwood
- Federico Fellini
- John Ford
- Jodie Foster
- Jean-Luc Godard
- F. Gary Gray
- D. W. Griffith
- Alice Guy-Blaché
- Howard Hawks
- Alfred Hitchcock
- Albert and Allen Hughes
- John Huston
- Buster Keaton
- Diane Keaton
- Stanley Kubrick
- Akira Kurosawa
- Fritz Lang
- Malcolm D. Lee
- Spike Lee
- Kasi Lemmons
- George Lucas
- Penny Marshall
- June Mathis
- Oscar Micheaux
- Tyler Perry
- Mary Pickford
- Roman Polanski
- Martin Scorsese
- John Singleton
- Steven Spielberg
- Barbra Streisand
- Quentin Tarantino
- George Tillman, Jr.
- Orson Welles
- Forest Whitaker
- Billy Wilder

....

Community Resources: Film professors, local film directors

....

Books:
Shaner, P., & Jones, G. E. (2004). *Digital filmmaking for teens*. Boston: Thomson Course Technology.

Shulman, M., & Krog, H. (2004). *Attack of the killer video book: Tips and tricks for young directors*. Toronto: Annick Press.

Web Sites:

Kids' Vid
http://kidsvid.altec.org
Instructional Web site for students and teachers regarding video production.

The Director in the Classroom
http://www.thedirectorintheclassroom.com
Web site for educators regarding how to engage students in learning through filmmaking.

Quotes to Inspire:

"The film industry is about saying 'no' to people, and inherently you cannot take 'no' for an answer."—James Cameron

"Perhaps it sounds ridiculous, but the best thing that young filmmakers should do is to get hold of a camera and some film and make a movie of any kind at all."—Stanley Kubrick

FILM PRODUCT GUIDE	
Components	**Exemplary Characteristics**
Acting	• Believable • Use of appropriate gestures and facial expressions • Well-rehearsed
Camera Work	• Steady and captures all important images • Appropriate and carefully planned camera positions, camera angles, and zooms
Lighting	• All images, important scenery, and props are clearly visible at all appropriate times • Appropriate modifications to the lighting have been made to enhance the images
Music/Score	• Appropriate to content, sets desired mood/tone • Complements and enhances subject matter • Appropriate use of tempos and volume to highlight important scenes and/or dialogue • Appropriate credits and/or copyright permissions secured
Narration (Optional)	• Effectively uses a variety of inflection, pace, and emotion • Innovatively incorporated

FILM PRODUCT GUIDE	
Screenplay	<ul><li>Thoughtfully scripted, shows details instead of telling them</li><li>Incorporates meaningful, "real" dialogue as appropriate that reveals the personality/traits of each character and demonstrates the differing values between characters, advances either the plot or the characterization, and helps progress the story</li><li>Includes detailed and thorough stage directions whose actions and descriptions are vivid and create visual pictures</li><li>Action advances plot</li><li>Adheres to all elements of format including margins, page numbers, sluglines, dialogue, and descriptions</li><li>Incorporates sophisticated transitions that build to climax</li></ul>
Sound	<ul><li>Crisp and smooth</li><li>Effectively corresponds with images</li><li>Background noise kept to a minimum</li></ul>
Special Effects/ Editing	<ul><li>Visual effects add interest and enhance the theme, not overstated</li><li>Edits are well-selected and promote flow and story development</li></ul>
Storyboard	<ul><li>Reflects thorough planning, fully developed, considers all elements of the project</li><li>Fluid and cohesive, follows a logical sequence</li><li>Presented in a manner that efficiently organizes all aspects of the project (transitions, special effects, sound, etc.)</li></ul>
Story/Theme	<ul><li>Interesting and engaging</li><li>All perspectives are thoroughly explored</li><li>Incorporates a compelling situation that is resolved in a realistic manner</li><li>Plot follows a logical, appropriately paced progression</li><li>Captures and maintains audience attention</li><li>Develops interesting characters</li></ul>

PRODUCT: GRAPHIC ORGANIZER

DEFINITION: A communication tool that uses visual symbols and/or images to convey ideas and concepts.

....

TITLES OF THE EXPERT: Teacher, graphic designer

....

TYPES OF GRAPHIC ORGANIZERS:

- Cause-Effect chart
- Classification chart
- Concept web
- Continuum scale
- Digital dashboard
- Euler diagram
- Flow chart
- Ishikawa (fishbone diagram)
- KWL chart
- Matrix
- Mind map
- Network tree
- Pie chart
- Series of events chain
- Sequence/Flow chart
- Spider map
- SQ3R chart
- Story map
- T-chart
- Thinking tree
- Timeline
- Two story map
- Venn diagram

....

WORDS TO KNOW:

- Analyze
- Brainstorm
- Classify
- Compare
- Contrast
- Evaluate
- Hierarchy
- Hypothesize
- Interact
- Linear
- Metacognition
- Mnemonic
- Nonlinear
- Radial
- Relationship
- Sequence
- Visualize

....

21ST-CENTURY SKILLS: Creativity and innovation skills, critical thinking and problem-solving skills, communication skills, information literacy, technology skills, flexibility and adaptability, interdisciplinary understanding, mastery of core subjects

Helpful Hints:

- When creating the graphic organizer, concentrate on the relationships between and among topics.
- Determine which parts of your idea/concept are the most important when placing information onto your graphic organizer.
- Choose the type/format of graphic organizer that best fits your topic and purpose.
- Always consider the audience when selecting a type/format of graphic organizer.

Exemplary Producers:

- Neville Brody
- Tony Buzan
- David Carson
- Walt Disney
- Leonhard Euler
- Frank Gilbreth
- Kaoru Ishikawa
- Ramon Llull
- Dmitri Ivanovich Mendeleev
- Joseph Novak
- Porphyry of Tyre
- John Venn

Community Resources: Teacher, graphic designer, business/marketing person

Books:

Hyerle, D. (1996). *Visual tools for constructing knowledge.* Alexandria, VA: Association for Supervision and Curriculum Development.

Inspiration Software, Inc. (2006). *Inspiration: Version 8, getting started.* Beaverton, OR: Author.

Web Sites:

ReadWriteThink—Graphic Map
http://www.readwritethink.org/materials/graphicmap
Interactive tool that allows users to create a graphic map.

Inspiration Software Tutorial
http://cf.inspiration.com/prodev/index.cfm?fuseaction=training
View comprehensive tutorials illustrating the key features of this visual thinking software.

QUOTES TO INSPIRE:

"A common mistake that people make when trying to design something completely foolproof is to underestimate the ingenuity of complete fools."—Douglas Adams

"Design is a plan for arranging elements in such a way as best to accomplish a particular purpose."—Charles Eames

GRAPHIC ORGANIZER PRODUCT GUIDE	
COMPONENTS	EXEMPLARY CHARACTERISTICS
Arrangement	• Logical • Succinctly presented, reflects essential information • Main concept easily identified • Subconcepts branch appropriately
Design	• Attractive, clean, and uniform • Effective use of color for emphasis • Selected fonts are easy to read
Graphics (Optional)	• Clear, crisp, and well situated on the page • Enhance comprehension
Relationships	• Clear and accurate • Linking lines connect related concepts in correct direction
Titles/Labels	• Neat • Prominent where appropriate • Appropriately placed • Correct spelling/grammar

PRODUCT: HANDBOOK

DEFINITION: A collection of instructions on any topic that is intended to provide ready reference.

TITLES OF THE EXPERT: Technical writer, handbook writer

TYPES OF HANDBOOKS:

- Company
- Employee/Student
- Field guide
- Pocket reference
- Scientific
- Style guides (writing)
- Survival guide
- Technical
- Travel

WORDS TO KNOW:

- Compendium
- Diagram
- Index
- Manual
- Policy
- Procedures
- Reference
- Table of contents
- Vade mecum

21ST-CENTURY SKILLS: Creativity and innovation skills, critical thinking and problem-solving skills, communication skills, collaboration skills, information literacy, technology skills, media literacy, flexibility and adaptability, initiative and self-direction, productivity and accountability, leadership and responsibility, interdisciplinary understanding, mastery of core subjects

HELPFUL HINTS:

- Customize your handbook for the intended audience.
- Include a comprehensive index and table of contents to make your handbook quick and easy to use.
- Clearly label topics and sections within the handbook so readers can easily locate desired information.
- Write in a clear and concise manner.

EXEMPLARY PRODUCERS:

- John James Audubon
- Eugene Fodor
- Michael "Mac" McCarthy
- John Muir
- Roger Tory Peterson
- Joshua Piven
- Dugald A. Steer
- Lynn Troyka

COMMUNITY RESOURCES:

Writing teachers, college professors, human resource personnel

BOOK:

Spencer, L. (2005). *A step-by-step guide to informative writing.* New York: Rosen.

WEB SITE:

ReadWriteThink—Printing Press
http://www.readwritethink.org/student_mat/student_material.asp?id=36
Interactive tool that allows users to create their own newspaper, flyer, brochure, or booklet.

QUOTE TO INSPIRE:

"If you don't find it in the index, look very carefully through the entire catalogue."
—Unknown

HANDBOOK PRODUCT GUIDE

Components	Exemplary Characteristics
Content	• Relevant • Thorough coverage of topic, provides all essential information to the reader, goes beyond the obvious or predictable
Cover	• Visually pleasing, attractive • Easy to read, title and author's name are clear and prominent • Font and colors are appropriate to content • Graphics and illustrations, if present, are eye-catching and are associated with handbook content
Graphics/Illustrations/ Diagrams (Optional)	• Clear, crisp, and well situated on the page • Enhance comprehension
Index	• Effectively guides reader to desired point in handbook • Comprehensive; includes key terms, concepts, events, places, and people • Developed with careful consideration of the audience and their desired use • Appropriately alphabetized
Mechanics	• Appropriate use of grammar • Free of spelling errors • Strong evidence of proofreading
Organization/ Navigation	• User friendly, information can be located with ease • Presented in a logical and organized manner • Effectively incorporates "finding aids" for reader (i.e., table of contents, index, tabs, headings, etc.)
Table of Contents	• Includes all entries in a neat, organized manner • Corresponds with appropriate page numbers • Easy to read

PRODUCT: HISTOGRAM

DEFINITION: A statistical graph showing frequency of data.

TITLE OF THE EXPERT: Statistician

TYPES OF HISTOGRAMS:

- Color
- Cumulative
- Image

WORDS TO KNOW:

- Bar graph
- Bin
- Categories
- Class
- Data
- Deviation
- Distribution
- Frequencies
- Intervals
- Measurement
- Skewed
- Variable

21ST-CENTURY SKILLS: Creativity and innovation skills, critical thinking and problem-solving skills, communication skills, information literacy, technology skills, media literacy, flexibility and adaptability, initiative and self-direction, mastery of core subjects

HELPFUL HINTS:

- Use your data to choose the right scale. Remember that all scales start at 0.
- Draw and label the scale on the vertical (up and down) axis first.
- Draw and label the horizontal axis next.
- List the name of each item.
- Draw vertical lines to represent each number.
- Remember that the vertical lines must touch.

EXEMPLARY PRODUCERS:

- David Blackwell
- George E. P. Box
- David R. Cox
- Gertrude Cox
- F. N. David
- Bradley Efron
- R. A. Fisher
- George Gallup
- Sir Francis Galton
- Margaret Jarman Hagood
- Florence Nightingale
- Janet Norwood
- Karl Pearson
- Donald Richards
- John Tukey
- Frank Yates

COMMUNITY RESOURCES: Math teachers, statistics professors

BOOKS:

Nechaev, M. W. (2004). *Making graphs.* Milwaukee, WI: Gareth Stevens.
Wingard-Nelson, R. (2004). *Data, graphing, and statistics.* Berkeley Heights,
    NJ: Enslow.

WEB SITE:

NCES Kids' Zone—Create a Graph
http://nces.ed.gov/nceskids/createagraph
Describes different types of graphs and how they are used and allows users to
create their own graphs.

QUOTES TO INSPIRE:

"While the individual man is an insoluble puzzle, in the aggregate he becomes a
mathematical certainty. You can, for example, never foretell what any one man
will be up to, but you can say with precision what an average number will be
up to. Individuals vary, but percentages remain constant. So says the statistician."—Sir Arthur Conan Doyle

"Not everything that can be counted counts; and not everything that counts can
be counted."—George Gallup

HISTOGRAM PRODUCT GUIDE	
COMPONENTS	EXEMPLARY CHARACTERISTICS
Appearance	• Well designed, neat, and attractive • Color, if used, is complementary and enhances readability
Axes	• Both the X and Y axes of the graph are clearly labeled
Bars	• Depict all relevant data • Accurate plotting of all points
Key	• Clearly defines the data • Effectively assists with interpretation of data • Positioned for ease of use
Title/Labels	• Representative of the content being graphed • Prominently and/or appropriately located • Labels are clear, neat, and appropriately descriptive of the related variable

PRODUCT: HOLOGRAM

DEFINITION: A flat surface that appears to contain a three-dimensional image.

TITLE OF THE EXPERT: Holographer

TYPES OF HOLOGRAMS:
- Animated
- Digital
- Embossed
- Multiplex (or cross)
- Pseudocolor
- Rainbow
- Reflection
- Transfer
- Transmission

WORDS TO KNOW:
- Beamsplitter
- Coherence
- Diffraction
- Interference pattern
- Laser
- Master hologram
- Object beam
- Phase
- Reference beam
- Wavelength
- White light

21ST-CENTURY SKILLS: Creativity and innovation skills, critical thinking and problem-solving skills, communication skills, collaboration skills, technology skills, media literacy, flexibility and adaptability, initiative and self-direction, productivity and accountability, mastery of core subjects

HELPFUL HINTS:
- Choose an object that is solid, inanimate, and white in color.
- Remember that vibrations and the smallest movement can ruin a hologram. Try to be completely still and quiet. Also, turn off any air conditioning or heating systems and any potential sources of vibrations.
- Be aware that not all lasers or laser pointers can be used to make holograms. It's best to choose a laser that has been pretested for meeting the required specifications.
- Never look directly into any laser beam.
- If you are using a processing kit, be very careful when handling any chemicals and follow all directions to the letter.
- Always seek the assistance of an experienced adult.

EXEMPLARY PRODUCERS:

- Stephen A. Benton
- Margaret Benyon
- Rudie Berkhout
- Harriet Casdin-Silver
- Lloyd Cross
- Paula Dawson
- Frank DeFreitas
- Yuri N. Denisyuk
- Mark Diamond
- Dennis Gabor
- Tung Jeong
- Victor Komar
- Emmett Leith
- Sam Moree
- Bruce Nauman
- Peter Nicholson
- Robert Powell
- Rich Rallison
- Carl Frederick Reutersward
- Jason Sapan
- Karl Stetson
- Juris Upatnieks

COMMUNITY RESOURCES: Science teacher, physics/computer professors

BOOK:

Kasper, J. E., & Feller, S. A. (2001). *The complete book of holograms: How they work and how to make them.* Mineola, NY: Dover Publications.

WEB SITES:

Holoworld.com
http://www.holoworld.com/holo/kids.html
A special page devoted to young students that explains holograms and their uses.

Holophile, Inc.
http://www.holophile.com
A company specializing in holography. Site includes comprehensive information on the history of holography.

Simple Holography
http://www.holokits.com/a-simple_holography.htm
Step-by-step instructions for making a simple hologram.

QUOTE TO INSPIRE:

"If we were to ask the brain how it would like to be treated, whether shaken at a random, irregular rate, or in a rhythmic, harmonious fashion, we can be sure that the brain, or for that matter the whole body, would prefer the latter. The implications of this holographic model are monumental. It implies that all the knowledge in the Universal Mind is available to anyone who can tune into it, because, as in all holograms, the information is totally distributed throughout the universe."—Itzhak Bentov

HOLOGRAM PRODUCT GUIDE	
COMPONENTS	EXEMPLARY CHARACTERISTICS
Image	• Three-dimensional • Shows depth and parallax • From every viewing angle you see the image in a different perspective • Every part of the hologram contains the whole image
Set-Up/Preparation	• Appropriate object is selected (i.e., solid, stable, bright when illuminated) • Employs effective methods for eliminating movement and vibration • Room is sufficiently darkened • Essential supplies secured (e.g., diode laser, holographic plates, processing kit)

PRODUCT: ILLUSTRATED STORY

DEFINITION: A general storybook layout with illustrations or pictures.

TITLES OF THE EXPERT: Author, writer, illustrator

TYPES OF ILLUSTRATED STORIES:

- Abstract picture
- Illustrated text
- Informal portrait
- Photo and text combination
- Picture story within text
- Pure picture story
- Single picture story

WORDS TO KNOW:

- Characters
- Description
- Detail
- Dialogue
- Fiction
- Layout
- Narrative
- Nonfiction
- Picture book
- Plot
- Setting
- Sketch
- Storyboard
- Text

21ST-CENTURY SKILLS: Creativity and innovation skills, critical thinking and problem-solving skills, communication skills, technology skills, initiative and self-direction, productivity and accountability, interdisciplinary understanding, mastery of core subjects

HELPFUL HINTS:

- Do a preliminary search for visual materials that you think may relate to your story. This will help you imagine your own illustrations.
- Notice the images and feelings that the story elicits and keep these in mind when creating your illustrations.
- Share ideas with friends and family about expressing your story visually.
- Select the materials you will need to produce the types of illustrations you desire.

EXEMPLARY PRODUCERS:

- Jan Brett
- Margaret Wise Brown
- Eric Carle
- Tomie dePaola
- Lois Ehlert
- Tom Feelings
- Pat Hutchins
- Crockett Johnson
- Ezra Jack Keats
- Leo Lionni
- Mercer Mayer
- David Macaulay
- Robert McCloskey
- Laura Numeroff
- Jerry Pinkney
- Patricia Polacco
- Beatrix Potter
- Robert Quackenbush
- H. A. Rey
- Faith Ringgold
- Michael Elsohn Ross
- Cynthia Rylant
- Ruth Sanderson
- Maurice Sendak
- Dr. Seuss (Theodor Seuss Geisel)
- Shel Silverstein
- Seymour Simon
- Peter Spier
- William Steig
- Nancy Tafuri
- Tasha Tudor
- Chris Van Allsburg
- David Wiesner
- Mo Willems
- Vera B. Williams
- Don Wood

COMMUNITY RESOURCES: Creative writing/Art teachers, local authors or illustrators

BOOKS:

Loewen, N. (2009). *Show me a story: Writing your own picture book.* Minneapolis, MN: Picture Window Books.

Melton, D. (1985). *Written & illustrated by—: A revolutionary two-brain approach for teaching students how to write and illustrate amazing books.* Kansas City, MO: Landmark Editions.

WEB SITES:

Bruce Hale—How to Write a Story
http://www.brucehale.com/howto.htm
Online tutorial by children's book author, Bruce Hale.

Writing With Writers
http://teacher.scholastic.com/writewit
Students work with writers, authors, and illustrators in workshops to help develop their writing skills.

Quotes to Inspire:
"'What is the use of a book,' thought Alice, 'without pictures or conversations?'"—Lewis Carroll

"There is more treasure in books than in all the pirates' loot on Treasure Island and best of all, you can enjoy these riches every day of your life."—Walt Disney

ILLUSTRATED STORY PRODUCT GUIDE	
Components	Exemplary Characteristics
Characters	• Vividly described (appearance and actions) • Fully developed • Interesting
Illustrations	• Enhance story and reader comprehension • Detailed, attractive, and imaginative • Relate to the text on the page • Age appropriate • Appropriate to tone of story
Mechanics	• Appropriate use of grammar • Free of spelling errors • Strong evidence of proofreading
Narration/Dialogue	• Effectively conveys mood • Incorporates rich language • Very readable • Appropriate to character's age, personality, and point of view; effectively brings the characters to life
Plot	• Well developed, detailed • Engaging beginning, draws the reader in, sparks interest • Fluid and coherent • Satisfying conclusion
Setting	• Vivid, descriptive • Enhances story • Conveys time, location, weather

PRODUCT: JEWELRY

DEFINITION: An item of personal adornment that is worn.

....

TITLES OF THE EXPERT: Jeweler, jewelry designer

....

TYPES OF JEWELRY:

• Beaded	• Fiber	• Stone
• Bone	• Glass	• Wire
• Clay	• Metal	• Wood

....

WORDS TO KNOW:

• Birthstone	• Facet	• Lapidary
• Cameo	• Faux	• Locket
• Carat	• Filigree	• Plated
• Clasp	• Finish	• Soldering
• Electroplate	• Gilt	• Vermeil
• Engraving	• Inclusion	

....

21ST-CENTURY SKILLS: Creativity and innovation skills, critical thinking and problem-solving skills, flexibility and adaptability, initiative and self-direction, productivity and accountability, mastery of core subjects

....

HELPFUL HINTS:

- Learn the basics of jewelry making first. Read books and craft magazines on the subject and check the Internet for information.
- Consider taking jewelry-making classes. Check bead/craft stores or community centers for available classes.
- Find a place where you can work and be creative as you make your jewelry.
- Organize your workspace. Cabinets with multiple small drawers work great for storing beads, fasteners, and other small jewelry supplies.
- Make sure you have the right tools on hand, such as needlenose pliers, flathead pliers, and wire cutters.

EXEMPLARY PRODUCERS:

- Sotirio Bulgari
- Alexander Calder
- Andréa Candela
- Jacques-Theodule Cartier
- Elsa Peretti
- Paloma Picasso
- Kara Ross

- Jean Schlumberger
- Vincenzo Taormina
- Louis Comfort Tiffany
- Dinh Van
- Harry Winston
- David Yurman

COMMUNITY RESOURCES: Local jeweler, jewelry artist, metalsmith

BOOKS:

Grisewood, S. (1995). *Making jewelry.* New York: Kingfisher Books.

McSwiney, S., Williams, P., Davies, C. C., & Davies, J. (2007). *The jewelry making handbook: Simple techniques and step-by-step projects.* London: Chartwell Books.

WEB SITES:

About.com—Jewelry Making
http://jewelrymaking.about.com/od/beginnerscorner/Beginners_Corner.htm
Archived articles and projects for beginning jewelry makers.

The Artist's Toolkit
http://www.artsconnected.org/toolkit
Watch visual demonstrations of the elements and principles of design.

QUOTES TO INSPIRE:

"The hues of the opal, the light of the diamond, are not to be seen if the eye is too near."—Ralph Waldo Emerson

"There is in them a softer fire than the ruby, there is the brilliant purple of the amethyst, and the sea green of the emerald—all shining together in incredible union. Some by their splendor rival the colors of the painters, others the flame of burning sulphur or of fire quickened by oil."—Pliny

JEWELRY PRODUCT GUIDE	
COMPONENTS	EXEMPLARY CHARACTERISTICS
Craftsmanship	• Demonstrates considerable attention to construction • All items are neatly trimmed and/or are carefully and securely attached. • For metal jewelry—the soldered seams meet well and are invisible. Finish is smooth with no blemishes or scratches • For fiber jewelry—the knots are uniformly tied and consistent • For beaded jewelry—There is a pattern and color scheme • Durable, can be put on and moved around without breaking or falling apart, built to last through multiple wearings or performances
Design/Appearance	• Attractive • Reveals excellent knowledge and understanding of the use of design elements (e.g., unity, contrast, balance, movement, direction, emphasis, and center of interest) • Style consistent with the techniques or art being studied • Appropriate size for intended wearer

PRODUCT: JOURNAL

DEFINITION: A written record of personal experiences and observations.

TITLES OF THE EXPERT: Journal writer, diarist

TYPES OF JOURNALS:

- Art
- Blog
- Creative
- Dialectical
- Dream
- Family
- Focused
- Gardening
- Gratitude
- Health
- Idea
- Lists
- Literary
- Media
- Metacognitive
- Nature
- Personal/Daily life
- Photo
- Pre-flective
- Progress journal
- Reflective
- Research
- Response
- Scientific
- Spending
- Spiritual
- Structured
- Study
- Team
- Thematic
- Therapy
- Travel

WORDS TO KNOW:

- Blogosphere
- Dialogue
- Diary
- Embellishment
- Excerpt
- Insight
- Interpretation
- Intuition
- Memoir
- Monologue
- Observation
- Point of view
- Posthumous
- Prompt
- Reflection
- Self-expression
- Twitter

21ST-CENTURY SKILLS: Creativity and innovation skills, critical thinking and problem-solving skills, communication skills, technology skills, media literacy, initiative and self-direction, productivity and accountability, mastery of core subjects

HELPFUL HINTS:

- Gather the items you will need to begin your journal. You may want to keep it simple and use just a blank book and a pen, or use a variety of craft items to create a more elaborate scrapbook-style journal.

- If using a paper to record your thoughts, select acid-free paper to ensure the pages are preserved over time.
- Think of your journal as a place to record anything that interests you and to experiment with thoughts and ideas.
- Keep your journal where you will remember to use it often.
- Be specific with names, dates, and places when you write journal entries. You will be glad you did when you read them again years later and no longer remember the exact details of every recorded experience.
- Think about creating an online version of your journal using a blog (Weblog), or keep a journal on your computer by saving it in any word processing program.

EXEMPLARY PRODUCERS:

- John Adams
- John Quincy Adams
- Louisa May Alcott
- Frances Burney
- Meg Cabot
- Lewis Carroll
- Henry Channon
- Mary Boykin Chesnut
- William Clark
- Richard Crossman
- Charles Darwin
- Leonardo da Vinci
- Albert Einstein
- Ralph Waldo Emerson
- Anne Frank
- Thomas Hardy
- Thomas Jefferson
- Carl Jung
- Frida Kahlo
- James Lees-Milne
- Meriwether Lewis
- Anne Morrow Lindbergh
- George Orwell
- George S. Patton
- Samuel Pepys
- Henry Crabb Robinson
- John Steinbeck
- George Templeton Strong
- Henry David Thoreau
- Leo Tolstoy
- Sophia Tolstoy
- Thomas Turner
- Mark Twain
- Virginia Woolf
- Dorothy Wordsworth

COMMUNITY RESOURCES: English/writing teacher, librarian

BOOKS:

Mirriam-Goldberg, C., Verdick, E., & Dreyer, D. (1999). *Write where you are: How to use writing to make sense of your life: A guide for teens.* Minneapolis, MN: Free Spirit.

Stevens, C. (1993). *A book of your own: Keeping a diary or journal.* New York: Clarion Books.

WEB SITE:

Scholastic's Dear Dumb Diary
http://www.scholastic.com/titles/deardumbdiary
Interactive tool with pointers for keeping a diary.

QUOTES TO INSPIRE:

"After the writer's death, reading his journal is like receiving a long letter."—Jean Cocteau

"When my journal appears, many statues must come down."—Arthur Wellesley

JOURNAL PRODUCT GUIDE	
COMPONENTS	EXEMPLARY CHARACTERISTICS
Content/Entries	• Relevant, presents important information • Detailed • Well-organized, follows a logical sequence • Demonstrates evidence of reflection, moves beyond summary of events • Convincing and realistic point of view
Cover	• Unique use of title and graphics • Attractive • Consistent with theme
Illustrations (optional)	• Detailed • Appropriately correspond to each entry
Mechanics (optional)	• Appropriate use of grammar • Free of spelling errors • Strong evidence of proofreading

PRODUCT: LOGIC PUZZLE

DEFINITION: A word problem that is solved through deduction or the process of elimination.

TITLES OF THE EXPERT: Logician, mathematician, puzzle maker

TYPES OF LOGIC PUZZLES:

- Fillomino
- Goishi Hiroi
- Grid
- Hashiwokakero
- Heyawake
- Hitori
- Hotaru Beam
- Induction
- Isolate
- Kakuro
- Kenken
- Knights and Knaves
- Lateral thinking
- Masyu
- Mochikoro
- Navigrid
- Nonogram
- Number link
- Oekaki
- Sudoku
- Survo
- Tatamibari
- Tatebo-Yokobo
- Three-way duel
- Unisol
- Yajilin
- Zebra

WORDS TO KNOW:

- Analysis
- Deduction
- Elimination
- Fallacy
- Fuzzy logic
- Grid
- Inclusion
- Maze
- Red herring
- Syllogism

21ST-CENTURY SKILLS: Creativity and innovation skills, critical thinking and problem-solving skills, communication skills, collaboration skills, technology skills, flexibility and adaptability, initiative and self-direction, productivity and accountability, mastery of core subjects

HELPFUL HINTS:

- Review examples of logic puzzles to get familiar with the various styles and formats.
- Keep in mind that the clues must give the reader enough information to solve the puzzle logically.
- Start with the solution and work backward.
- Write a detailed scenario that is concise, clear, and will engage readers.

- The more clues or attributes you provide, the greater the complexity your puzzle will have.
- Create a solution grid and double-check your work.
- Try your completed problem out on a friend.

EXEMPLARY PRODUCERS:

- Dave Barry
- Lewis Carroll
- Barry Clarke
- Henry Ernest Dudeney
- Albert Einstein
- Leonardo Fibonacci
- Martin Gardner
- Howard Garns
- Thomas Kirkman
- Sam Loyd
- Edouard Lucas
- Erno Rubik
- Will Shortz
- Raymond Smullyan

COMMUNITY RESOURCES: Math teacher, professional puzzle maker

BOOKS:

Buxton, M. L. R. (2007). *Math logic mysteries: Mathematical problem solving with deductive reasoning.* Waco, TX: Prufrock Press.

Clarke, B. (2003). *Challenging logic puzzles.* New York: Sterling.

WEB SITES:

Brainbashers Logic Puzzles
http://www.brainbashers.com/logic.asp
A collection of logic puzzles ranging in difficulty.

The Logic Problems Page
http://www.geocities.com/Heartland/Plains/4484/logic.htm
An abundance of information related to logic puzzles from how to create them to where to find them.

Mystery Master Logic Puzzles
http://www.mysterymaster.com/puzzles.html
A Web site designed to help solve logic puzzles.

QUOTES TO INSPIRE:

"When you have eliminated the impossible, whatever remains, however improbable, must be the truth."—Sherlock Holmes

"A good puzzle, it's a fair thing. Nobody is lying. It's very clear, and the problem depends just on you."— Erno Rubik

LOGIC PUZZLE PRODUCT GUIDE	
COMPONENTS	EXEMPLARY CHARACTERISTICS
Clues	• Provide just enough information for the problem to be solved, do not directly reveal answer • Clearly written • Woven into story/scenario • Relate only to content of story/scenario, no outside knowledge required
Matrix/Solving Grid (Optional)	• Matches information in puzzle • Clearly labeled
Scenario/ Problem	• Entertaining • Original • Well-developed • Concise and clear, unambiguous, easy to follow • Results in one logical solution that satisfies the problem and all the clues

PRODUCT: MASK

DEFINITION: A cover, or partial cover, for the face, used for disguise or protection.

TITLES OF THE EXPERT: Mask maker, artist, costume designer

TYPES OF MASKS:

- Bauta
- Buccal
- Bugaku
- Burial
- Carnival
- Ceremonial
- Commedia
- Disguise
- Facial
- Fashion
- Festival
- Functional
- Funeral
- Gas
- Gigaku
- Gladiator
- Gnaga
- Gyodo
- Halloween
- Mardi Gras
- Moretta
- Noh
- Occupational
- Opera
- Performance
- Portrait
- Protective
- Ritual
- Segoni-kun
- Spirit
- Sports
- Theatrical
- Tupeng

WORDS TO KNOW:

- Accoutrement
- Anthropomorphic
- Archetypes
- Balaclava
- Caricature
- Carving
- Coiffure
- Comic
- Disguise
- Drama
- Exaggeration
- Expression
- Folklore
- Gilded
- Harlequin
- Impersonate
- Kachina
- Lacquer
- Masque
- Masquerade
- Papier-mâché
- Persona
- Satire
- Symbolic
- Symmetry
- Theriomorphic

21ST-CENTURY SKILLS: Creativity and innovation skills, critical thinking and problem-solving skills, communication skills, flexibility and adaptability, initiative and self-direction, productivity and accountability, interdisciplinary understanding, mastery of core subjects

HELPFUL HINTS:

- For beginners, an asymmetrical rather than symmetrical mask is recommended.
- Be sure to give plenty of height to the eyeholes for adequate vision.
- If painting the mask, make use of shading as this can add dramatic effect.
- Select the lightest materials possible to construct your mask.
- Embellish the mask as appropriate using feathers, ribbon, beads, and other materials.
- Be creative and express your individuality in your mask.

EXEMPLARY PRODUCERS:

- Torbjörn Alström
- W. T. Benda
- George Bettelyoun
- Juan Horta Castillo
- Dolores Purdy Corcoran
- Bob Frith
- Brian Froud
- Wendy Froud
- Zarco Guerrero
- David K. John
- Beckie Kravetz
- Jerry Laktonen
- Fannie Loretto
- Merced Maldonado
- Katy Marchant
- Bruce Marrs
- Lillian Pitt
- Victoriano Salgado
- Donato Sartori
- Oskar Schlemmer
- Becky Olvera Schultz
- Jeff Semmerling
- Stanley Allan Sherman
- Lula Vassoureiro
- Ernest Whiteman

COMMUNITY RESOURCES: Art teacher, local mask maker, theatre director, costume designer

BOOKS:

D'Cruz, A. M. (2009). *Make your own masks.* New York: PowerKids Press.
Schwarz, R. (2002). *Making masks.* Toronto: Kids Can Press.

WEB SITES:

Another Face: Masks Around the World
http://gallery.sjsu.edu/masks/Homefram.html
Interactive site that provides background information about masks and has a gallery of many images.

PBS Kids Go! Africa for Kids
http://pbskids.org/africa/mask
Information and patterns for making African masks.

....

QUOTES TO INSPIRE:
"Man is least himself when he talks in his own person. Give him a mask, and he will tell you the truth."—Oscar Wilde

"Without wearing any mask we are conscious of, we have a special face for each friend."—Oliver Wendell Holmes

MASK PRODUCT GUIDE	
COMPONENTS	EXEMPLARY CHARACTERISTICS
Craftsmanship	• Carefully planned and designed • Demonstrates considerable attention to construction, all items are neatly trimmed and/or are carefully and securely attached • Sturdy, built to withstand multiple wearings or performances
Form	• Conveys appropriate emotion/mood • Details are all easily viewed and identifiable from a distance
Function (Optional)	• Comfortable • Practical, wearer's vision is not obstructed

PRODUCT: MOSAIC

DEFINITION: An art form where small pieces of rock, tile, shell, glass, paper, or other materials are fitted together to create an abstract or representational design.

TITLES OF THE EXPERT: Mosaicist, artist

TYPES OF MOSAICS:
- Ceramic
- Glass
- Paper
- Photo
- Slate
- Stone
- Tile

WORDS TO KNOW:
- Adhesive
- Andamento
- Ciottoli
- Direct method
- Double indirect method
- Grout
- Gummed paper
- Indirect method
- Inlay
- Interstices
- Mounting grid
- Opus musivum
- Opus palladianum
- Opus regulatum
- Opus tessellatum
- Opus vermiculatum
- Smalti
- Tesserae
- Tile glue
- Tile mesh
- Tile nippers

21ST-CENTURY SKILLS: Creativity and innovation skills, critical thinking and problem-solving skills, flexibility and adaptability, initiative and self-direction, productivity and accountability, interdisciplinary understanding, mastery of core subjects

HELPFUL HINTS:
- Use a simple design for your mosaic pattern. Basic designs like the ones in coloring books work best.
- Break up larger tiles into smaller pieces by putting them in a bag and smashing them with a hammer a few times.

- Choose colored grout instead of white to add a more polished look to your work.
- Always wear eye protection when cutting or breaking tile.
- Wear gloves to protect your hands from sharp tile edges while you work.
- Use concrete board rather than plywood as a base for your mosaic. Tiles will not stick to plywood over a long period of time.
- Keep the grout damp as it cures to prevent crumbling.

....

EXEMPLARY PRODUCERS:

- Seymour Adelman
- Giovanni Battista Calandra
- Alexandra Carron
- Raffaelle Castellini
- Fabio Cristofari
- Pietro Paolo Cristofari
- Giandomenico Facchina
- Gaddo Gaddi
- Michele Giambono
- Leon D. Harmon
- Maurice Richard Josey
- Sarah Kelly
- Kenneth C. Knowlton
- Hildreth Meière
- Jason Mercier
- Melinda Moore
- Ludwig Oppenheimer
- Angelo Orsoni
- Proclus
- Marcello Provenzale
- Matteo Randi
- Saimir Strati
- Leonid Stroganov
- Isaiah Zagar

....

COMMUNITY RESOURCES: Art teacher, local mosaic artist

....

BOOKS:

Massey, P., & Slater, A. (1999). *Beginner's guide to mosaic*. Tunbridge Wells, UK: Search.

Powell, M. (2001). *Mosaics*. Tunbridge Wells, UK: Search.

....

WEB SITES:

Mosaic Atlas
http://www.mosaicatlas.com
A resource for sharing photos of public mosaic sites from around the world.

Mosaic Matters
http://www.mosaicmatters.co.uk
Online magazine for all things mosaic.

QUOTES TO INSPIRE:
"Winter is an etching, spring a watercolor, summer an oil painting and autumn a mosaic of them all."—Stanley Horowitz

"Each of us puts in one little stone, and then you get a great mosaic at the end."—Alice Paul

MOSAIC PRODUCT GUIDE	
COMPONENTS	EXEMPLARY CHARACTERISTICS
Craftsmanship	• Exquisitely constructed; demonstrates considerable attention to precision; all items are neatly spaced, trimmed, and carefully and securely attached • Crisp, clear layout of pieces; content easily viewed and identified
Design/Appearance	• Applies design principles (i.e., color, repetition, balance, etc.) in a unique and complementary manner; effectively used to establish a focal point • Ambitious, original, interesting, and/or thoughtful composition; highly detailed • Evidence of careful planning

PRODUCT: MUSICAL COMPOSITION

DEFINITION: A piece of original music designed for performance.

TITLE OF THE EXPERT: COMPOSER, MUSICIAN, MAESTRO

TYPES OF MUSICAL COMPOSITIONS:

- Canon
- Cantata
- Capriccio
- Concerto
- Dance
- Duet
- Electronic
- Étude
- Fantasia
- Fugue
- Glee
- Hymn
- Instrumental
- Mixed
- Nocturne
- Nonet
- Octet
- Opera
- Oratorio
- Overture
- Parody
- Pastoral
- Prelude
- Requiem
- Rhapsody
- Septet
- Sextet
- Sonata
- Suite
- Symphony
- Trio
- Quartet

WORDS TO KNOW:

- Adagio
- Allegro
- Aria
- Arrangement
- Atonality
- Cadence
- Chorale
- Chord
- Clef
- Da capo
- Dissonance
- Encore
- Ensemble
- Finale
- Harmony
- Impromptu
- Key
- Melody
- Notation
- Opus
- Refrain
- Rhythm
- Tempo
- Tone
- Treble
- Tune
- Vivace

21ST-CENTURY SKILLS: Creativity and innovation skills, critical thinking and problem-solving skills, communication skills, flexibility and adaptability, initiative and self-direction, productivity and accountability, leadership and responsibility, interdisciplinary understanding, mastery of core subjects

HELPFUL HINTS:
- Play your music for friends or family members who know something about music and get their opinions about it.
- Start with a rough draft just like you would in English class. Music needs rewriting several times before the final draft is complete.
- Listen to other composers' music to learn techniques and tricks you may not know.

EXEMPLARY PRODUCERS:
- Louis Armstrong
- Johann Sebastian Bach
- Amy Beach
- Ludwig van Beethoven
- Vincenzo Bellini
- Leonard Bernstein
- Johannes Brahms
- Francesca Caccini
- Teresa Carreño
- Francesco Cavalli
- Cécile Chaminade
- Frédéric Chopin
- Aaron Copland
- John Coltrane
- Antonín Dvořák
- Edward K. "Duke" Ellington
- George Gershwin
- Stan Getz
- Dizzy Gillespie
- Benny Goodman
- Christoph Willibald Gluck
- Georg Friedrich Händel
- Franz Joseph Haydn
- Fanny Mendelssohn Hensel
- Elisabeth-Claude Jacquet de la Guerre
- Gustav Mahler
- Henry Mancini
- William Mason
- Felix Mendelssohn
- Wolfgang Amadeus Mozart
- Florence Beatrice Price
- Giacomo Puccini
- Gioacchino Antonio Rossini
- Alma Schindler
- Arnold Schoenberg
- Franz Peter Schubert
- Clara Wieck Schumann
- Igor Stravinsky
- Germaine Tailleferre
- Ilya Tchaikovsky
- Antonio Vivaldi
- Giuseppe Verdi
- Hildegard von Bingen
- Richard Wagner

COMMUNITY RESOURCES: Music teacher, college professor, local musician

BOOKS:

Balodis, F. (2001). *Young composer's notebook: A student's guide to composing.* Mississauga, Ontario: Frederick Harris Music.

Wilson, J. (2005). *Composition for young musicians: A fun way for kids to begin creating music.* Van Nuys, CA: Alfred.

Web Sites:

Creating Music
http://www.creatingmusic.com
Online creative music environment where kids can compose.

SFS Kids—Fun With Music
http://www.sfskids.org
Interactive site for kids from the San Francisco Symphony that explores music and instruments.

Quotes to Inspire:

"There's nothing remarkable about it. All one has to do is hit the right keys at the right time and the instrument plays itself."—Johann Sebastian Bach

"Though everything else may appear shallow and repulsive, even the smallest task in music is so absorbing, and carries us so far away from town, country, earth, and all worldly things, that it is truly a blessed gift of God."—Felix Mendelssohn

MUSICAL COMPOSITION PRODUCT GUIDE	
COMPONENTS	EXEMPLARY CHARACTERISTICS
Elements	**Rhythm** • All measures have the correct number of beats • Variety of rhythms and variance of patterns are used • Clear and compelling • Consistently accurate and appropriate, balance is maintained throughout **Melody (if appropriate)** • Extremely clear • Well-established, consistent throughout • Not repetitious, variety of contour and phrasing **Harmony (if appropriate)** • Well-articulated • Variety of texture • Consonant, blending of pitches
Performance (Optional)	• Strong aesthetic appeal • Varied, keeps the listener interested • Effectively achieves the composer's intended effect
Score/Notation	• Adheres to standard notational conventions • Includes all required elements (title, instrument, clef sign, time signature, key signature, etc.) • Written neatly using proper bar line placement • Correctly notated for the appropriate voice or instruments

PRODUCT: NEEDLECRAFT

DEFINITION: Canvas work assembled with yarn or thread and a needle.

TITLE OF THE EXPERT: Needlecrafter

TYPES OF NEEDLEWORK:
- Applique
- Candlewicking
- Crewel
- Crochet
- Cross stitch
- Embroidery
- Knitting
- Lacemaking
- Macramé
- Needle felting
- Needlepoint
- Passementerie
- Punch needle
- Quilting
- Sewing
- Smocking
- Stitchery
- Tapestry
- Tatting
- Weaving

WORDS TO KNOW:
- Aida cloth
- Basketweave
- Basting
- Canvas
- Continental
- Embroidery hoop
- Fabric
- Floss
- French knot
- Half cross
- Hardanger
- Loom
- Petit point
- Ply
- Quarter stitch
- Rug canvas
- Sampler
- Scroll frame
- Skein
- Tent stitch
- Tweeding

21ST-CENTURY SKILLS:
Creativity and innovation skills, critical thinking and problem-solving skills, flexibility and adaptability, initiative and self-direction, productivity and accountability, mastery of core subjects

HELPFUL HINTS:
- Create a contrast in color and value between the focal point and the background.
- Working thread sheets should be 18–20 inches long.
- The needle selected should fit through the mesh of the canvas without having to push or pull.
- It is always better to stitch the smaller areas of the design before the larger ones.

- When you are finishing a thread, don't pull too hard because it will make your last stitch pucker.
- For the beginner, needlecraft kits are recommended as they come with instructions, designs, and all of the supplies you will need.

EXEMPLARY PRODUCERS:

- Reem Acra
- Young Yang Chung
- Leon Conrad
- Kaffe Fassett
- Charles Germain de Saint-Aubin
- Mary Morris Knowles
- Donna Kooler
- Hans Krondahl
- Marilyn Leavitt-Imblum
- Ann Macbeth
- May Morris
- Anna Mary Robertson Moses (Grandma Moses)
- Betsy Ross
- Anna Brita Sergel
- Wendela Gustafva Sparre
- Alice Starmore
- Gustava Johanna Stenborg
- Teresa Wentzler
- Erica Wilson
- Elizabeth Zimmerman

COMMUNITY RESOURCES: Local needlecrafters, quilters, textile artists

BOOKS:

Gibson, R., Castor, H., Wheatley, M., Young, N., & Moller, R. (2005). *Starting needlecraft*. London: Usborne.

Sadler, J., Kinsler, G. B., & Young, J. (2005). *The jumbo book of needlecrafts*. Toronto: Kids Can Press.

WEB SITES:

Learn to Knit and Crochet
http://www.learntocrochet.com/home.html
Learn the basics and peruse project ideas.

Wonderful Stitches
http://www.needlework.com
An array of resources for stitchery enthusiasts.

QUOTE TO INSPIRE:

"Take your needle, my child, and work at your pattern; it will come out a rose by and by. Life is like that—one stitch at a time taken patiently and the pattern will come out all right like the embroidery."—Oliver Wendell Holmes

NEEDLECRAFT PRODUCT GUIDE	
COMPONENTS	EXEMPLARY CHARACTERISTICS
Craftsmanship/ Overall Appearance	• Neat, stitches are well organized • Knots or thread/yarn ends are clipped and not visible • Project is well constructed
Design	• Applies design principles (i.e., color, repetition, balance, etc.) in a unique and complementary manner; effectively used to establish a focal point • Ambitious, original, interesting, and/or thoughtful composition; highly detailed
Stitches	• Secure and tight • Uniform in size • Accurate, begin and end in the same direction • Consistently executed

PRODUCT: ORIGAMI

DEFINITION: The Japanese art of folding paper into representational shapes or objects.

TITLE OF THE EXPERT: Origamist

TYPES OF ORIGAMI:

- Abstract
- Action
- Ancient
- Classic
- Complex
- Composite
- Compound
- Digital
- Fabric
- Geometric
- Golden Venture
- Kirigami
- Knotology
- Modular
- Multimodular
- Noshi
- Pop-up
- Pureland
- Simple
- Single sheet
- Storigami
- Tear-i-gami
- Technical
- Traditional
- Unit

WORDS TO KNOW:

- Assembly
- Base
- Bird base
- Blintz fold
- Box-pleating
- Closed sink
- Closed unsink
- Collapse
- Crease
- Crimp fold
- Double open sink
- Eccentric
- Faceted
- Fish base
- Frog base
- Inside reverse fold
- Kami
- Kirigami
- Kite base
- Mountain fold
- Open sink
- Outside reverse fold
- Pentagon
- Petal fold
- Pleat fold
- Preliminary fold
- Rabbit ear fold
- Radial pleat fold
- Sink
- Soft fold
- Spread squash
- Squash fold
- Swivel fold
- Tessellation
- Twist fold
- Unsink
- Valley fold
- Washi
- Waterbomb base
- Wet-folding

21ST-CENTURY SKILLS: Creativity and innovation skills, critical thinking and problem-solving skills, flexibility and adaptability, initiative and self-direction, productivity and accountability, interdisciplinary understanding, mastery of core subjects

Helpful Hints:

- Get started with any kind of paper. There is no need to purchase expensive paper at first. Office paper works fine, or try gift wrap and candy wrappers.
- Wash your hands before you fold to prevent soiling the paper.
- Learn the basic folds first.
- Using paper that is colored differently on each size helps to distinguish the front from the back when following directions.
- Fold each crease precisely and flatten well.
- Follow the instructions very carefully. Your project will be much more difficult otherwise.
- Be patient. Learning origami takes time and practice.

Exemplary Producers:

- Jeff Beynon
- Dave Brill
- Roman Diaz
- Peter Engel
- Lin Fengmian
- Tomoko Fuse
- Eric Gjerde
- Robert Harbin
- Kunihiko Kasahara
- Rachel Katz
- Kenneth Kawamura
- Robert J. Lang
- John Montroll
- Jeannine Mosely
- Vicente Palacios
- Nick Robinson
- Jeremy Shafer
- Florence Temko
- Joseph Wu
- Makoto Yamaguchi
- Akira Yoshizawa

Community Resources: Art teacher, local origamist

Books:

Boonyadhistarn, T. (2007). *Origami: The fun and funky art of paper folding.* Mankato, MN: Capstone Press.

Boursin, D. (2007). *Folding for fun.* Richmond Hill, Ontario: Firefly Books.

O'Brien, E., & Needham, K. (2007). *Origami and other paper projects.* Tulsa, OK: Usborne Books.

Web Sites:

Oriland

http://www.oriland.com

The biggest and most imaginative paper world ever!

Origami With Rachel Katz

http://www.origamiwithrachelkatz.com

An overview of common origami paper symbols and folds.

QUOTE TO INSPIRE:
"Some people are peculiarly susceptible to the charms of origami, and somewhere along the way the ranks of the infected were joined by mathematicians."—Robert J. Lang

ORIGAMI PRODUCT GUIDE	
COMPONENTS	EXEMPLARY CHARACTERISTICS
Craftsmanship	• Folds are clean with crisp creases, little or no wrinkles • Lasting, can be handled without needing immediate repair • Presentable, obvious attention to detail
Design	• Ambitious, original, interesting, and/or thoughtful composition • Highly detailed, complex • Paper (i.e., thickness, texture, color, etc.) is appropriate to the structure • Functions as intended (action origami)
Directions/Instructions	• Clearly written • Use professional terminology • Correct punctuation and grammar • Easy to understand • Drawings/photos of the steps are accurate and aid construction (optional)

PRODUCT: PETITION

DEFINITION: A written request seeking action that is presented to someone of authority.

TITLE OF THE EXPERT: Petitioner

TYPES OF PETITIONS:
- Online (modern)
- Paper (traditional)

WORDS TO KNOW:
- Appeal
- Authority
- Ballot
- Cause
- Citizen
- e-Signatures
- Grievance
- Issue
- Jurisdiction
- Lobby
- Ordinance
- Persuasion
- Pleading
- Protocol
- Sponsor
- Target

21ST-CENTURY SKILLS: Global awareness; financial, economic, and/or business literacy; entrepreneurial literacy; civic literacy; critical thinking and problem-solving skills; communication skills; collaboration skills; information literacy; technology skills; initiative and self-direction; social and cross-cultural skills; productivity and accountability; leadership and responsibility; interdisciplinary understanding; mastery of core subjects

HELPFUL HINTS:
- Find out from local government offices if you need a permit to petition in your area. Secure permissions for those premises that you wish to use as petition sites.
- Write your petition statement clearly and concisely—get straight to the point, so potential signers know at a glance what you are trying to accomplish.
- Be polite when asking for signatures.
- If using an online petition, use Internet tools such as blogs, e-mail, and discussion groups to reach a wide audience.

EXEMPLARY PRODUCERS:

- Susan B. Anthony
- Frédéric Bastiat
- Barbara Boxer
- Pierre-Joseph Cambon
- Sir Edward Coke
- John Dickinson
- Alfred Domett
- John Hancock
- Margaret Higinbotham
- Thomas Jefferson
- Oliver St. John
- Bessie Lee
- Jane Munro
- Johan van Oldenbarnevelt
- Gloria Richardson
- Ernestine Louise Rose

COMMUNITY RESOURCES: Teacher, local attorney

BOOKS:

Hoose, P. M. (1993). *It's our world, too!: Stories of young people who are making a difference.* New York: Little, Brown.

Lewis, B. A. (2004). *The kid's guide to social action: How to solve the social problems you choose—and turn creative thinking into positive action.* Minneapolis, MN: Free Spirit.

WEB SITE:

GoPetition
http://www.gopetition.com
Offers support on how to write a petition.

QUOTES TO INSPIRE:

"The Normans came over, lance in hand, burning and trampling down every thing before them, and cutting off the Saxon dynasty and the Saxon nobles at the edge of the sword; but the right of petition remained untouched."—Caleb Cushing

PETITION PRODUCT GUIDE	
COMPONENTS	EXEMPLARY CHARACTERISTICS
Body	• Open, honest, and to-the-point • Elaborates the purpose of the petition • Provides clear explanations and valid reasons to support intentions
Conclusion	• Provides clear and valid reasons why respondents should support/sign petition • Validates readers' impact, ensures readers that their support matters and can make a difference
Format/Presentation	• Professional, of high quality • Well-presented, neat and organized • Signature pages use a format that is easy to see, easy to fill in, and easy to review
Introduction	• Captures readers' attention • Efficiently outlines the contents of the proposal
Purpose/Call-to-Action	• Substantiated; thoroughly researched; data is accurate, current, and supportive of argument • Clear and concise • Appeals to target

PRODUCT: PHOTO ESSAY

DEFINITION: A series of photographs, usually accompanied by written text, that are placed in a specific order to convey a story.

TITLE OF THE EXPERT: Photographer, photojournalist

TYPES OF PHOTO ESSAYS:

- Chronology/Time sequence
- Contrast
- Event
- How-to
- Idea
- Location
- Narrative
- Repetition
- Thematic

WORDS TO KNOW:

- Caption
- Close-up
- Cropping
- Detail photo
- Ethics
- Installation art
- Layout
- Lead photo
- Mixed media
- Montage
- Newsworthy
- Portrait
- Scene
- Signature photo

21ST-CENTURY SKILLS: Creativity and innovation skills, critical thinking and problem-solving skills, communication skills, information literacy, technology skills, media literacy, flexibility and adaptability, initiative and self-direction, productivity and accountability, interdisciplinary understanding, mastery of core subjects

HELPFUL HINTS:

- Pick a subject that you are interested in and care about.
- Look for the story behind the story. An interesting angle will make your essay more interesting and memorable.
- Use your essay to connect with the audience through emotions that relate to everyone's daily lives.
- Plan out each photo in your essay ahead of time. Think of each photo as a sentence in the story you want to tell.

EXEMPLARY PRODUCERS:

- Eddie Adams
- Diane Arbus
- Margaret Bourke-White
- Mathew B. Brady
- Milbert Orlando Brown
- Robert Capa
- Henri Cartier-Bresson
- Bruce Davidson
- Alfred Eisenstaedt
- Walker Evans
- Kevin Fleming
- Mark Gail
- Lauren Greenfield
- Carol Guzy
- Charles "Teenie" Harris
- Stan Honda
- Joachim Ladefoged
- Dorothea Lange
- Peter J. Menzel
- James Nachtwey
- Gordon Parks
- Lucian Perkins
- Dith Pran
- Alexander M. Rivera
- W. Eugene Smith
- Carol Szathmari
- Dixie D. Vereen
- Homai Vyarawalla
- Ernest Withers

COMMUNITY RESOURCES: Photography teacher or college professor, local photojournalist

BOOKS:

Osiecki, L., & Hoogstraten, S. (1995). *How to create a photo essay.* Morristown, NJ: Silver Burdett Ginn.

Schulke, F. (2003). *Witness to our times: My life as a photojournalist.* Chicago: Cricket Books.

WEB SITES:

National Press Photographer's Association
http://www.nppa.org
Association dedicated to the advancement of visual journalism.

5 Photo Essay Tips
http://digital-photography-school.com/5-photo-essay-tips
Helpful tips from a photo journalist.

QUOTES TO INSPIRE:

"We don't make a photograph just with a camera, we bring to the act of photography all the books we have read, the movies we have seen, the music we have heard, the people we have loved."—Ansel Adams

"Sometimes I enjoy just photographing the surface because I think it can be as revealing as going to the heart of the matter."—Annie Leibovitz

PHOTO ESSAY PRODUCT GUIDE	
COMPONENTS	EXEMPLARY CHARACTERISTICS
Captions	• Succinct and expressive • Clear, describe what is happening so viewer can understand • Contain informational content as appropriate
Essay	• Strong and compelling, responds in great depth to what is conveyed in the photographs, thought-provoking • Well-written, free of grammar and spelling errors • Leaves the reader thinking
Photos	• Varied in presentation (e.g., wide-angled, detailed, portraits, etc.) • Arranged in a logical and interesting sequence • Selected with care and precision; each photo contributes to the overall story, theme, and/or emotions of the essay • Meaningful and informative, relevant to the context • Evoke emotion • Objective, fair and accurate depiction of events • High quality, compositionally and artistically strong, could stand alone without written component

PRODUCT: PODCAST

DEFINITION: An audio or video broadcast available on the Internet.

TITLE OF THE EXPERT: Podcaster

TYPES OF PODCASTS:
- Audio
- Enhanced
- Video

WORDS TO KNOW:
- Aggregator
- Bandwidth
- Broadcast
- Channel
- Mash
- Media RSS
- Mixing board
- Mobcast
- MP3
- Narrowcast
- Newsfeed
- Peer cast
- Photofeed
- Podcatcher
- Punchcast
- Skypecast
- Slivercast
- Stinger
- Streaming media
- Syndication
- Triplecast
- Unicast
- Web feed
- XLM
- Zencasting

21ST-CENTURY SKILLS: Creativity and innovation skills, critical thinking and problem-solving skills, communication skills, collaboration skills, information literacy, technology skills, media literacy, flexibility and adaptability, initiative and self-direction, social and cross-cultural skills, productivity and accountability, leadership and responsibility, interdisciplinary understanding, mastery of core subjects

HELPFUL HINTS:
- Use a high-quality microphone.
- Record your podcast in a room with good acoustics that is free from distracting environmental noises.
- Position your microphone correctly—not too close or too distant from your mouth.
- Prepare what you want to say ahead of time, but do not read from a script.

- Record your podcasts on a regular schedule.
- Try using background music to add interest.

EXEMPLARY PRODUCERS:

- Jay Berkowitz
- Dan Carlin
- Adam Curry
- Natali Del Conte
- Tim Devine

- Michael Geoghegan
- Ricky Gervais
- Dan Klass
- Mur Lafferty
- Leo Laporte

- Cliff Ravenscraft
- Nathan Rose
- Evo Terra

COMMUNITY RESOURCES: Computer teacher, local podcaster

BOOKS:

Richardson, W. (2009). *Blogs, wikis, podcasts, and other powerful web tools for classrooms.* Thousand Oaks, CA: Corwin Press.

Sawyer, S. (2008). *Career building through podcasting.* New York: Rosen.

WEB SITES:

Kid-Cast.com
http://www.kid-cast.com
A Web site for kids to publish their own podcasts for other kids.

How to Podcast
http://www.how-to-podcast-tutorial.com
Step-by-step podcast tutorial.

QUOTE TO INSPIRE:

"After about nine months of building up the momentum, I figured, OK, now I'm gonna commercialize it. Podcasting is a lot more difficult than dashing off a post on a weblog. Podcasts take time. You have to record and create in real time, and invest more time editing. . . . So with podcasting, now there's an opportunity for anyone to create [an] audio show and distribute it worldwide, efficiently."—Adam Curry

PODCAST PRODUCT GUIDE	
COMPONENTS	EXEMPLARY CHARACTERISTICS
Content	• Appropriate, well-researched and informative • Establishes a clear purpose • Engages the listener immediately
Delivery	• Well-rehearsed, smooth delivery in a conversational style; not reliant on a script • Clear and intelligible, words are effectively enunciated • Expression and rhythm enhance experience for the listener • Appropriate volume
Supplemental Graphics and/or Music (Optional)	• Enhance presentation • Permissions for use of copyright material have been obtained and appropriately documented
Technical Aspects	• Sections are organized clearly and cohesively • Microphone positioned appropriately • Free of distracting background noises • Appropriate length for intended audience

PRODUCT: POP-UP BOOK

DEFINITION: A book that contains one or more pages in which a three-dimensional structure rises up when a page is opened.

TITLES OF THE EXPERT: Paper engineer, author, writer, artist

TYPES OF POP-UP BOOKS:

- Dissolving disc
- Double page
- Fanfolded
- Lift-the-flap
- Mechanical
- Metamorphoses
- Moveable
- Peek-a-boo
- Pop-outs
- Pull-downs
- Pull-tabs
- Transformations
- Tunnel
- Volvelles

WORDS TO KNOW:

- 90° element
- 180° element
- Action book
- Base page
- Battledore
- Cardstock
- Carousel
- Coil
- Die-cut
- Gate fold
- Harlequinade
- Illusion
- Panorama
- Perspective
- Tagboard
- Transformation
- Wheel

21ST-CENTURY SKILLS: Creativity and innovation skills, critical thinking and problem-solving skills, communication skills, information literacy, technology skills, flexibility and adaptability, initiative and self-direction, productivity and accountability, interdisciplinary understanding, mastery of core subjects

HELPFUL HINTS:

- Begin by using premade templates for practice.
- Sketch out your idea first.
- Practice using scissors by making snowflakes or paper dolls until cutting becomes comfortable.
- Work on one page at a time.
- When gluing, let each page dry completely.

EXEMPLARY PRODUCERS:

- Carol Barton
- David A. Carter
- Roger Culbertson
- S. Louis Giraud
- Theo Gielen
- Mark Hiner
- Waldo Hunt
- Vojtech Kubasta
- Harold B. Lentz
- Ramon Llull
- Luciana Mancosu
- Lothar Meggendorfer
- Ann Montanaro
- Ernest Nister
- Kyle Olmon
- Jan Pienkowski
- Matthew Reinhart
- Ellen G. K. Rubin
- Robert Sabuda

COMMUNITY RESOURCES: English/writing teacher, local author, artist

BOOKS:

Diehn, G. (2006). *Making books that fly, fold, wrap, hide, pop up, twist, & turn.* New York: Lark Books.

Stowell, C., & Robins, J. (1994). *Making books.* New York: Kingfisher Books.

WEB SITES:

Joan Irvine: How to Make a Pop-Up
http://www.makersgallery.com/joanirvine/howto.html
Excerpted from her book, *How to Make Pop-ups.*

Robert Sabuda—Simple Pop-Ups You Can Make!
http://robertsabuda.com/popmake/index.asp
Simple pop-ups you can make.

Mark Hiner—Paper Engineer
http://www.markhiner.co.uk
History, samples, and tips for making pop-ups.

QUOTE TO INSPIRE:

"Mechanical books should look like ordinary books. Their success is to be measured by the ingenuity with which their bookish format conceals unbookish characteristics."—Iona and Peter Opie

POP-UP BOOK PRODUCT GUIDE

Components	Exemplary Characteristics
Craftsmanship	• Sturdy and durable, pop-ups are securely attached to the book to withstand regular use and manipulation • Of professional quality overall • High-quality paper used for book pages • Artistic; pop-ups are carefully drawn, colored, and cut out • All parts work as intended
Mechanics	• Free of spelling and/or grammar errors
Pictures/Illustrations	• Neat, carefully drawn • Appropriately sized • Design/layout corresponds and enhances story/text
Story/Text	• Engaging beginning, draws the reader in, sparks interest • Incorporates rich language • Well-developed, detailed • Fluid and coherent • Satisfying conclusion

PRODUCT: PROTOTYPE

DEFINITION: A preliminary, rudimentary model or design usually made for demonstration purposes.

TITLES OF THE EXPERT: Designer, inventor, engineer, prototyping specialist

TYPES OF PROTOTYPES:

- Alpha
- Beta
- Conceptual
- Custom fabricated
- Form, fit, and function
- Form study
- Functional
- Performance
- Physical
- Proof-of-principle
- Virtual
- Visual

WORDS TO KNOW:

- Archetype
- Example
- First
- Mock-up
- Model
- Original
- Paradigm
- Precedent
- Proof of concept
- Scale
- Simulation
- Standard

21ST-CENTURY SKILLS: Financial, economic, and/or business literacy; entrepreneurial literacy; creativity and innovation skills; critical thinking and problem-solving skills; communication skills; collaboration skills; information literacy; technology skills; media literacy; flexibility and adaptability; initiative and self-direction; productivity and accountability; leadership and responsibility; interdisciplinary understanding; mastery of core subjects

HELPFUL HINTS:

- Brainstorm an invention of some kind that you would like to create.
- Make rough versions of your prototype using inexpensive household items to get an idea of how your prototype might work.
- Have friends or family members test out your prototype to see what they think.

EXEMPLARY PRODUCERS:

- Scott Amron
- Alexander Graham Bell
- Josephine Garis Cochrane
- Samuel Colt
- Leonardo da Vinci
- John Deere
- Walt Disney
- James Dyson
- Thomas Edison
- Albert Einstein
- Henry Ford
- Benjamin Franklin
- Galileo Galilei
- Bill Gates
- Charles Goodyear
- Robert William Kearns
- Guglielmo Marconi
- Elizabeth Messer
- Sir Isaac Newton
- Norbert Rillieux
- Earl S. Tupper
- Orville Wright
- Wilbur Wright
- Frank Lloyd Wright

COMMUNITY RESOURCES: Local inventors

BOOKS:

Casey, S. (2005). *Kids inventing!: A handbook for young inventors*. Hoboken, NJ: John Wiley.

Salvadori, M. (1990). *The art of construction: Projects and principles for beginning engineers and architects*. Chicago: Chicago Review Press.

WEB SITES:

About.com—Making a Prototype
http://inventors.about.com/od/prototypes/a/prototype.htm
List procedures and legal considerations for making a prototype.

From Patent to Profit
http://www.frompatenttoprofit.com/prototypes.htm
An invention education company.

QUOTES TO INSPIRE:

"Building a prototype proves your concept will work as suggested. It could be big and ugly, as long as it works."—Andrew Wythes

"Every building is a prototype. No two are alike."—Helmut Jahn

PROTOTYPE
PRODUCT GUIDE

Components	Exemplary Characteristics
Appearance/Design	<ul><li>Demonstrates thorough understanding of the problem and design criteria</li><li>Selected scale is appropriate to product and purpose</li><li>Appropriately demonstrates form, fit, and/or function</li><li>Effectively and accurately represents concept/product</li><li>Obvious that considerable time has been given to the design</li><li>Easy to understand/use</li></ul>
Construction	<ul><li>Clean, nicely organized/presented</li><li>Well-made</li><li>Appropriate materials were selected, functional</li><li>Economical, materials are accessible and affordable</li><li>Demonstrates thorough understanding of the properties of selected materials</li></ul>
Function	<ul><li>Functions as intended, performs all necessary functions for demonstrating concept/product</li><li>Durable, withstands repetitive manipulation and/or testing</li><li>Evidence of testing and troubleshooting to resolve potential problems</li></ul>
Plan/Blueprint	<ul><li>Neat</li><li>Clear and accurate measurements</li><li>All components correctly labeled</li></ul>

PRODUCT: QUESTIONNAIRE

DEFINITION: A set of questions specifically designed to gather information.

TITLES OF THE EXPERT: Interviewer, market researcher, social researcher

TYPES OF QUESTIONNAIRES:

- E-mail
- Face-to-face
- Focus group
- Group-administered
- In-house survey
- Internet
- Mail
- Mall intercept
- Semistructured
- Structured
- Telephone
- Unstructured

WORDS TO KNOW:

- Anchors
- Anonymity
- Attitudes
- Close-ended
- Confidentiality
- Content analysis
- Demographic
- Dichotomous
- Likert scale
- Media exposure
- Open-ended
- Opinions
- Random
- Reliability
- Response rate
- Sample
- Significance
- Statistics
- Stratified
- Survey
- Validity

21ST-CENTURY SKILLS: Civic literacy, communication skills, collaboration skills, information literacy, technology skills, initiative and self-direction, social and cross-cultural skills, productivity and accountability, leadership and responsibility, interdisciplinary understanding, mastery of core subjects

HELPFUL HINTS:

- Provide clear instructions that detail how to complete the questionnaire.
- Make sure the questions included on your questionnaire will get the type of information you are seeking from respondents.
- Keep in mind that open-ended questions will generate longer responses and are much more difficult to code and aggregate across a large group.
- Avoid leading questions that direct respondents to a preferred answer, ambiguous questions that are open to different interpretations, and questions that seek more than one answer/response.
- The response options provided for each question should be mutually exclusive so that only one answer applies.

- Order your questions in a logical sequence. Group related questions together.
- Take care in the design of your questionnaire. Use a typeface that is easy to read and make use of sufficient white space to enhance readability.
- Streamline your questionnaire as much as possible by determining which questions are essential and most relevant to your purpose. Brevity will increase the likelihood that respondents will complete the questionnaire.
- Have friends and family complete the questionnaire first. This will help pinpoint any potential problems with your questionnaire before distributing to a wider audience.
- Remember to always thank your respondents.

EXEMPLARY PRODUCERS:

- Katharine Cook Briggs
- Raymond Cattell
- George Gallup
- Sir Francis Galton
- Louis Harris
- David Keirsey
- Paulina F. Kernberg
- Jon A. Krosnick

- Isabel Briggs Myers
- Arthur Charles Nielsen, Sr.
- Marcel Proust
- Elmo Roper
- Samuel A. Stouffer
- Seymour Sudman
- Lewis Terman
- Brian Wansink

COMMUNITY RESOURCES: Writing teacher, college or university researcher

BOOK:

Bradburn, N. M., Sudman, S., & Wansink, B. (2004). *Asking questions: The definitive guide to questionnaire design—For market research, political polls, and social and health questionnaires.* San Francisco: Jossey-Bass.

WEB SITE:

Creating a Questionnaire
http://writing.colostate.edu/guides/research/survey/com4a2.cfm
Writing guides for survey research created by Colorado State University.

QUOTES TO INSPIRE:
"Everyone takes surveys. Whoever makes a statement about human behavior has engaged in a survey of some sort."—Andrew Greeley

"If every day a man takes orders in silence from an incompetent superior, if every day he solemnly performs ritual acts which he privately finds ridiculous, if he unhesitatingly gives answers to questionnaires which are contrary to his real opinions and is prepared to deny his own self in public, if he sees no difficulty in feigning sympathy or even affection where, in fact, he feels only indifference or aversion, it still does not mean that he has entirely lost the use of one of the basic human senses, namely, the sense of humiliation."—Vaclav Havel

QUESTIONNAIRE PRODUCT GUIDE

COMPONENTS	EXEMPLARY CHARACTERISTICS
Appearance	• Professional • Crisp and clean, minimalist
Invitation Message/ Instructions	• Clearly written • Provides purpose for questionnaire • Identifies how information collected will be used • Prominently displayed so they are the first thing respondents see/read
Questions	• Clear, unambiguous • Aligned with/related to purpose • Appropriately grouped and sequenced • Adequate in number, enough to obtain desired information without being excessive • Free of spelling/grammar errors
Scale/Choices (Optional)	• Clear, mutually exclusive, and exhaustive • Scale/choices are appropriate for the question and audience

PRODUCT: QUILT

DEFINITION: A large cloth made from small fabric pieces sewn together in a creative and artistic manner.

TITLE OF THE EXPERT: Quilter

TYPES OF QUILTS:

- Album
- Amish
- Art
- Broderie perse
- Computer
- Crazy
- Foundation piecing
- Friendship
- Fused
- Hand
- Machine
- Medallion
- Memory
- Patchwork
- Pictorial
- Ralli
- Sashiko
- Signature
- Tivaivai
- Traditional
- Trapunto
- Watercolor
- Whole cloth

WORDS TO KNOW:

- Applique
- Backing
- Bargello
- Basting
- Batiks
- Batting
- Betweens
- Block
- Border
- Calico
- Chain piecing
- Cornerstones
- Cross-hatching
- Cutting mat
- Design
- Fat quarter
- Grain
- Homespun
- Lining
- Novelty prints
- Prairie points
- Rotary cutter
- Sampler
- Seam ripper
- Selvage
- Tacking
- Template
- Zinger

21ST-CENTURY SKILLS: Creativity and innovation skills, critical thinking and problem-solving skills, collaboration skills, flexibility and adaptability, initiative and self-direction, productivity and accountability, interdisciplinary understanding, mastery of core subjects

HELPFUL HINTS:

- Draw inspiration for your quilt design from the world around you. Nature is a great source for color ideas.

- Vary the texture and colors of your fabric to add interest.
- Remember to wash and dry your fabric before you begin.
- Always be sure to iron your fabric nice and flat.
- Buy more fabric than your pattern requires in case of mistakes.
- Try quilting with your friends to make it even more enjoyable.

EXEMPLARY PRODUCERS:

- Bob Adams
- Alex Anderson
- Esterita Austin
- Ellen Harding Baker
- Elizabeth Barton
- Phil Beaver
- Cuesta Benberry
- Sue Benner
- Mozell Benson
- Janet Catherine Berlo
- Sandy Bonsib
- Barbara Brackman
- Karen Kay Buckley
- Pauline Burbidge
- Elsie Campbell
- Hollis Chatelain
- Jennifer Chiaverini
- Jane Burch Cochran
- Karen Combs
- Nancy Crow
- Mimi Dietrich
- Carol Doak
- Radka Donnell
- Carol Bryer Fallert
- Kaffe Fassett
- Flavin Glover
- Beth Gutcheon
- Gloria Hansen
- Harriet Hargrave
- Susan Hoffman
- Michael James
- Jean Ray Laury
- Libby Lehman
- M. Joan Lintault
- Judy Martin
- Katie Pasquini Masopust
- Judy Mathieson
- Grace McCance
- Marsha McCloskey
- Marti Mitchell
- Miriam Nathan-Roberts
- Paula Nadelstern
- Harriet Powers
- Faith Ringgold
- Pam RuBert
- Patricia Stoddard
- Mary Rockhold Teter
- Rosie Lee Tompkins
- Molly Upton
- Marie Webster
- Joen Wolfrom

COMMUNITY RESOURCES: Local quilters, fabric store employees, college and university textile historians

BOOKS:

Stapleton, D. (2004). *Kids can quilt: Fun and easy projects for your small quilter.* Hauppauge, NY: Barron's.

Storms, B., & Bradford, J. (2001). *Quilting.* Toronto: Kids Can Press.

WEB SITES:

Quilting With Children
http://www.thecraftstudio.com/qwc
Site developed by a teacher who has been quilting with her students for years.

The Art of Quilting
http://www.pbs.org/americaquilts
Honors America's contemporary art quilters.

QUOTE TO INSPIRE:
"Take your needle, my child, and work at your pattern; it will come out a rose by and by. Life is like that—one stitch at a time taken patiently and the pattern will come out all right like the embroidery."—Oliver Wendell Holmes

QUILT PRODUCT GUIDE	
COMPONENTS	EXEMPLARY CHARACTERISTICS
Craftsmanship	• Of high quality • Shows considerable attention to construction • Neatly trimmed • All items are carefully and securely attached to the backing • Demonstrates precise sewing and cutting skills
Design/Appearance	• Appropriately applies design principles (such as unity, contrast, balance, movement, direction, emphasis, and center of interest) with great skill • Attractive and visually pleasing pattern • Neat, pressed flat
Theme/Concept	• Every item in the quilt clearly relates to the selected theme/concept

PRODUCT: RECIPE

DEFINITION: A set of directions for preparing something.

TITLES OF THE EXPERT: Cook, chef, food critic, culinary expert

TYPES OF RECIPES:

- Appetizer
- Beverage
- Bread, cake, and pie (pastry)
- Breakfast
- Candy
- Cookie
- Dessert
- International
- Main course (entrée)
- Salad
- Sandwich
- Sauces
- Seasonal and holiday
- Side dish
- Soup
- Vegetarian

WORDS TO KNOW:

- À la mode
- Al dente
- Baste
- Beat
- Blanch
- Boil
- Braise
- Butterfly
- Calorie
- Caramelize
- Chop
- Conversion
- Cube
- Cure
- Dash
- Dice
- Drain
- Dredge
- Fillet
- Garnish
- Grate
- Grease
- Grill
- Julienne
- Knead
- Marble
- Marinate
- Mince
- Mix
- Parboil
- Pare
- Pinch
- Poach
- Preheat
- Puree
- Reduce
- Roast
- Rounded
- Sauté
- Scald
- Scant
- Score
- Sear
- Season
- Shred
- Sieve
- Simmer
- Skewer
- Smoke
- Stir
- Steam
- Stew
- Temper
- Tenderize
- Toss
- Whip
- Whisk
- Zest

21ST-CENTURY SKILLS: Creativity and innovation skills, critical thinking and problem-solving skills, communication skills, information literacy, technology skills, flexibility and adaptability, Initiative and self-direction, productivity and accountability, interdisciplinary understanding, mastery of core subjects

HELPFUL HINTS:

- For original recipes, look for basic food compatibilities and standard cooking times.
- Learn about the many different spices and seasonings and their appropriate uses.
- Be precise; provide accurate amounts/quantities and descriptions of ingredients.
- Indicate potential ingredient substitutions that can vary the recipe.
- Write instructions in a clear and concise manner. Don't assume the reader is familiar with all cooking terms.
- Provide ideas for other dishes that might accompany or go well with your recipe.
- Remember to test your recipes to make sure they work, the amounts and serving sizes are correct, and that they taste as great as you intend.
- Have other people try out your recipes to see if they actually make sense.
- Make sure that all ingredients used are listed and that all ingredients listed are used.
- Read cookbooks from popular authors for inspiration. If you adapt a recipe from another source, be sure to give credit.

EXEMPLARY PRODUCERS:

- Sunny Anderson
- Mario Batali
- James Beard
- Raymond Blanc
- Anthony Bourdain
- Caesar Cardini
- Julia Child
- Jeff Cooks
- Helen Corbitt
- Martino da Como
- Paula Deen
- Rocco DiSpirito
- Fanny Farmer
- Debbi Fields
- Guy Fieri
- Bobby Flay
- G. Garvin
- Bert Greene
- Vertamae Grosvenor
- Augustus Jackson
- Emeril Lagasse
- Nigella Lawson
- Edna Lewis
- Mithaecus
- Sara Moulton
- Jamie Oliver
- Simone Ortega
- Paul Prudhomme
- Wolfgang Puck
- Gordon Ramsay
- Rachael Ray
- Harland Sanders (Colonel Sanders)
- Jeff Smith
- Martha Stewart

COMMUNITY RESOURCES: Cooking/home economics teacher, local chefs, family members, bakers

BOOKS:

Lagasse, E. (2004). *Emeril's there's a chef in my family!: Recipes to get everybody cooking.* New York: HarperCollins.

Wilkes, A. (2000). *The children's step-by-step cookbook.* New York: DK.

WEB SITES:

Writing Recipes

http://www.cookingupfun.cornell.edu/teachingguides/writingrecipes.html
Guidelines for writing and editing recipes from Cornell University's Division of Nutritional Services.

The Recipe Writer's Handbook

http://www.recipewritershandbook.com
An online manual for food professionals.

QUOTES TO INSPIRE:

"I feel a recipe is only a theme, which an intelligent cook can play each time with a variation."—Madame Benoit

"Omit and substitute! That's how recipes should be written. Please don't ever get so hung up on published recipes that you forget that you can omit and substitute."—Jeff Smith

RECIPE PRODUCT GUIDE	
COMPONENTS	EXEMPLARY CHARACTERISTICS
Appearance/Mechanics	• Neat • Correct spelling and grammar
Directions/Instructions	• Clear, step-by-step instructions presented in a logical sequence; easy to follow/understand • Specific cooking times and temperatures are noted • Photos/illustrations used to enhance understanding of procedures (optional) • Accurate number of servings recipe yields
List of Ingredients	• Clearly representative of theme/topic • Presented in order of use • Accurate measurements/amounts
Name/Title	• Appropriate, representative of ingredients and/or theme/topic

PRODUCT: SCRAPBOOK

DEFINITION: A book in which memorabilia and photos are collected and arranged.

....

TITLES OF THE EXPERT: Scrapbooker, scrapper

....

TYPES OF SCRAPBOOKS:
- Biographic/ autobiographic
- Digital
- Heritage
- Historical
- Journal

....

WORDS TO KNOW:
- Acid-free
- Archival mist
- Chipboard
- Clip art
- Collage
- Craft knife
- Crop
- Cutting mat
- Die-cutting
- Distressing
- Embellishment
- Emboss
- Font
- Mat
- Memorabilia
- Mosaic
- Page pocket
- Photo-safe adhesives
- Ribbon and fibers
- Scissors
- Shabby chic
- Shape punchers
- Sheet protectors
- Slide cutter
- Stamps
- Stencils
- Stickers
- Transparency
- Vellum
- Versamark

....

21ST-CENTURY SKILLS: Creativity and innovation skills, critical thinking and problem-solving skills, communication skills, information literacy, technology skills, media literacy, flexibility and adaptability, initiative and self-direction, productivity and accountability, interdisciplinary understanding, mastery of core subjects

....

HELPFUL HINTS:
- Add a premade envelope to your pages to provide a place to store extra bits of material related to your theme.
- For different looking titles for your pages, try using patterned paper for your cut-out letters.
- Use different fonts in your page titles to add a sense of fun to the page.

- To make a personalized background sheet that relates to a certain event in your scrapbook, take your official documents (wedding license, birth certificate, etc.), and make a photocopy or scan of them and then print them out on background paper.
- Before buying your first set of scrapbook supplies, do your research and talk with other scrapbookers to get a good idea of what supplies you really need.
- Save leftover paper. Even the smallest scraps may be used to embellish pages within your scrapbook.
- To prevent paper items like programs, ticket stubs, and notes from becoming brittle over time in your scrapbook, you can use an acid-free spray on them that will neutralize the acid and help preserve them for much longer.
- To protect your photos, look for photo-safe materials when you buy supplies, so they will not damage your photos.
- Choose a focal point photo or image.
- Mat your photos to make them stand out.
- Use other scrapbook pages in magazines and books to help you decide where to place your photos, title, and embellishments.

EXEMPLARY PRODUCERS:

- Lisa Bearnson
- Lewis Carroll
- Marielen Christensen
- Annie Grace Clarke
- John Day
- James H. DeVotie
- Ali Edwards
- Robert Allan "Fitz" Fitzgerald
- Elsie Flannigan
- Brendan Fraser
- Buckminster "Bucky" Fuller
- Jessica Helfand
- Becky Higgins
- Thomas Jefferson
- Mitchell Kraft
- Lucy Maud Montgomery
- Emma Louise Saxton Pascoe
- Angie Pedersen
- John Poole
- Mark Twain
- Cathy Zielske

COMMUNITY RESOURCES: Local scrapbookers or cardmakers, graphic artist, art teacher

BOOKS:

Meier, R. (2007). *Scrapbooking techniques for beginners.* New York: Sterling.

Pedersen, A. (2002). *The book of me: A guide to scrapbooking about yourself.* St. Louis, MO: EFG.

WEB SITES:

The Lewis Carroll Scrapbook Collection
http://international.loc.gov/intldl/carrollhtml/lchome.html
Browse through the pages of this author's scrapbook housed in the Library of Congress.

How to Start a Scrapbook
http://www.wikihow.com/Start-a-Scrapbook
Guidelines and tips for creating a scrapbook.

ScrapbooksEtc.com
http://www.scrapbooksetc.com
This site offers free tutorials, digital downloads, and lots of examples for getting started.

QUOTES TO INSPIRE:

"Arrange whatever pieces come your way."—Virginia Woolf

"If you don't know your family's history, then you don't know anything. You are a leaf that doesn't know it is part of a tree."—Michael Crichton

SCRAPBOOK PRODUCT GUIDE

Components	Exemplary Characteristics
Appearance/Design	• Highly attractive and eye catching. • Well-organized, the layout and design are of the highest quality • Space, shapes, textures, and colors selected add to the overall effectiveness of the scrapbook • The cover clearly identifies the theme, the theme is consistent throughout, all items in the scrapbook are relevant to the topic
Construction/ Craftsmanship	• All items are neatly trimmed • All items are carefully secured with appropriate quantity and quality of adhesive
Graphics/Photos/ Embellishments	• Complement the text • Well-balanced and appropriately arranged, a good mix of text and graphics/photos • Effectively cropped, trimmed, and/or matted for enhancement • Add to the overall effectiveness/theme of the scrapbook • Secured with enough adhesive of the proper type • Effectively spaced/arranged on page
Memorabilia/ Ephemera	• Secured with enough adhesive of the proper type • Appropriately treated/presented for prolonged life • Properly cited • Effectively spaced/arranged on page • The relationship of the item to the theme is evident
Titles/Labels/Text	• Well-written, clear, easy to read from adequate distance • Relevant and explanatory • Varied in color, size, and/or style for desired emphasis • Correctly correspond to graphics, photos, or embellishments • Proper grammar and spelling

PRODUCT: SERVICE PROJECT

DEFINITION: A planned, organized, and voluntary effort designed to address a problem or need within one's school, community, state, or the world.

TITLES OF THE EXPERT: Volunteer, humanitarian, activist

TYPES OF SERVICE PROJECTS:

- Advocacy
- Direct (face-to-face)
- Environmental
- Health and safety related
- Hunger and poverty
- Indirect experience
- In-school
- Intergenerational
- Community-based research

WORDS TO KNOW:

- Action research
- Beneficiary
- Capacity building
- Character education
- Civic responsibility
- Community
- Diversity
- Entrepreneurship
- Experiential education
- Mentoring
- Reciprocal partnerships
- Reflection
- Social capital
- Volunteerism

21ST-CENTURY SKILLS: Creativity and innovation skills, critical thinking and problem-solving skills, communication skills, collaboration skills, technology skills, media literacy, flexibility and adaptability, initiative and self-direction, social and cross-cultural skills, productivity and accountability, leadership and responsibility, interdisciplinary understanding, mastery of core subjects

HELPFUL HINTS:

- Plan ahead by talking with community leaders, teachers, and parents about the needs within your community.
- Remember that careful planning will maximize the chance of success.
- Recruit others to increase the impact of your project.
- Set reasonable goals and a realistic timeframe in which to accomplish them.

- Develop a plan to meet a specific need, and then determine what resources you have and will need to complete your goal.
- Keep track of your project along the way and evaluate the results after it is finished.

....

EXEMPLARY PRODUCERS:

- Jane Addams
- Carol Bellamy
- Richard Branson
- John Brown
- George H. W. Bush
- Jimmy Carter
- César Chávez
- Bill Clinton
- Harry Connick, Jr.
- Jean Henri Dunant
- Millard Fuller
- Peter Gabriel
- Bill and Melinda Gates
- Al Gore
- Albert Belmont Graham
- Paul Percy Harris
- Paul David Hewson (Bono)
- Bob Hope
- Hubert H. Humphrey
- Melvin Jones
- John F. Kennedy
- Martin Luther King, Jr.
- Wendy Kopp
- Jerry Lewis
- Michael J. McGivney
- Florence Nightingale
- Barack Obama
- Brad Pitt
- Franklin D. Roosevelt
- Elizabeth Cady Stanton
- Mother Teresa
- Harriet Tubman
- Desmond Tutu
- Ann Margaret Veneman
- Oprah Winfrey

....

COMMUNITY RESOURCES: Local charities and service organizations, local churches

....

BOOKS:

Lewis, B. A. (1995). *The kid's guide to service projects: Over 500 service ideas for young people who want to make a difference.* Minneapolis, MN: Free Spirit.

Lewis, B. A. (2005). *What do you stand for? For teens: A guide to building character.* Minneapolis, MN: Free Spirit.

Poplau, R. W. (2004). *The doer of good becomes good: A primer on volunteerism.* Lanham, MD: Scarecrow Education.

Web Sites:

Do Something
http://www.dosomething.org
A great place to begin when looking for some ideas on how to best serve your community.

Learn and Serve America
http://www.learnandserve.org
A comprehensive Web site covering all dimensions of service learning.

Quotes to Inspire:

"The best way to find yourself is to lose yourself in the service of others."—Mahatma Gandhi

"Only a life lived for others is a life worthwhile."—Albert Einstein

SERVICE PROJECT PRODUCT GUIDE	
COMPONENTS	EXEMPLARY CHARACTERISTICS
Engagement/ Implementation	• Well-organized • Participated in all activities, contributed to each step of the process • Active, direct collaboration with community
Goals/Purpose	• Clearly articulated to all involved • Proposed solution facilitates change or insight, solves the identified problem • Establishes a realistic timeline for project completion • Feasible, adequate resources are available (e.g., budget, materials, manpower, etc.)
Needs Assessment (Identifying the Problem)	• Identified barriers/problems based on thorough research/assessment • Problem discovered by student with little to no assistance from teacher
Reflection/Evaluation	• Thoughtful, addresses what he or she learned from the project • Connects experience with relevant academic content • Acknowledges areas that could be enhanced/ improved, includes detailed examples to support idea/conclusions • Demonstrates thorough knowledge of project area • Reveals deep personal understanding of the importance of service • Secures enough pertinent data to measure effectiveness and guide improvement, considers feedback from all participants
Value and Relevancy to Community	• Responds to actual community need that is recognized by the community, high value to the community as a whole or the group to which project is focused • Meets a need or addresses an important issue

PRODUCT: SPREADSHEET

DEFINITION: A grid effective for manipulating data (numerical or textual) that consists of cells containing labels, values, or a formula.

TITLES OF THE EXPERT: Accountant, researcher, statistician

TYPES OF SPREADSHEETS:

- Computer
- Diagonal matrix
- Logical
- Matrix
- Multidimensional
- Paper
- Scalar
- Symmetric matrix
- Table
- Vector

WORDS TO KNOW:

- Absolute cell reference
- Active cell
- Autosum
- Boolean operators
- Cell
- Charts
- Circular cell reference
- Column
- Data
- Entry bar
- Fill
- Formula
- Function
- Graphs
- Grid lines
- Macros
- Name box
- Number format
- Operators
- Range
- Relative cell reference
- Row
- Sheet tab
- Sort
- Statistics
- Tab
- Values
- Workbook
- Worksheet

21ST-CENTURY SKILLS: Critical thinking and problem-solving skills, communication skills, collaboration skills, technology skills, initiative and self-direction, productivity and accountability, leadership and responsibility, interdisciplinary understanding, mastery of core subjects

HELPFUL HINTS:

- Use the tab key to navigate between cells.
- The "=" symbol is used before all operations.
- Remember some symbols for operations are different when using a spreadsheet. For example "3 x 5" is written as "=3*5" on a spreadsheet.
- To add the contents of a group of cells, use the Σ button on the toolbar.

- Remember that when you type text into a particular cell, the words may appear to spread out into other cells, but they actually are all still in the original cell.
- The appearance of your spreadsheet can be changed by making columns wider or narrower.
- You can click on the letter or number tab on top (or on the right) of a column or row to select the entire column or row and change the font, size, or style of anything in the column.
- Click on the left-align, right-align, or center-align buttons to line up the text in that column, or use the "$" button on the toolbar to format any numbers as currency.
- You can create multiple charts from the same data or different data on a single worksheet.

EXEMPLARY PRODUCERS:

- David Blackwell
- Dan Bricklin
- Harry N. Cantrell
- Gertrude M. Cox
- Miguel de Icaza
- Russell E. Edwards

- A. Leroy Ellison
- Robert Frankston
- Dan Fylstra
- Bill Gates
- Mitch Kapor
- Remy Landau

- Richard Mattessich
- Rene K. Pardo
- Jonathan Sachs
- Kirstine Smith

COMMUNITY RESOURCES: Computer/office technology teacher

BOOKS:

Gipp, J. (2008). *Spotlight on spreadsheets.* Boston: Thomson/Course Technology.
Rooney, A. (2005). *Spreadsheets, graphs and charts.* London: QED.

WEB SITES:

Excel Simulations
http://aitt.acadiau.ca/tutorials/Excel2000/Excel2000simulations
Online tutorial for using Microsoft Excel.

Exploring Data
http://exploringdata.cqu.edu.au
Curriculum support materials for introductory statistics.

QUOTE TO INSPIRE:
"If they have those basic skills, like doing a spreadsheet, or just typing on the computer, then that's something they can use to get a job, and a better one than just going to work in some fast-food place."—Dave Sevick

SPREADSHEET PRODUCT GUIDE	
COMPONENTS	EXEMPLARY CHARACTERISTICS
Appearance/Format	• Exceptionally well-designed, neat, and attractive • Well-organized, clearly understood and interpreted • Use of complementary colors to make the graph more readable • Appropriate use of borders and shading to highlight important information • Fonts are set at a readable size and style • Alignment is consistent
Data Entry	• Complete and accurate • Corresponds with correct rows and columns • Organized in a manner that denotes relationships between data
Formulas	• Accurate, compute as intended • Located in appropriate cells
Graphs (Optional)	• Contain a title, labels, and a legend • Effective use of color for appeal • Appropriate for displayed data • Show trends and patterns
Headings/Labels	• Distinguishable from data and title • Appropriately label the data • Correct spelling
Title	• Appropriate to data/information • Prominent, distinguishable from data and headings/labels

PRODUCT: TERRARIUM

DEFINITION: An enclosed container in which living plants or animals are kept for display or observation.

TITLES OF THE EXPERT: Ecologist, gardener, landscaper, horticulturist

TYPES OF TERRARIUMS:

- Animal
- Biosphere
- Closed environment
- Desert
- Ecosphere
- Formicarium/ formicary
- Insectarium
- Open-air
- Paludarium
- Rainforest
- Riparium
- Vivarium
- Wardian case

WORDS TO KNOW:

- Aerate
- Annuals
- Aquatic plants
- Bonsai
- Bract
- Bromeliad
- Bulb
- Compost
- Cultivate
- Cuttings
- Decompose
- Dividing
- Dormancy
- Ecosystem
- Epiphyte
- Evaporation
- Fauna
- Flora
- Germinate
- Horticultural charcoal
- Humidity
- Hydroponics
- Organic matter
- Pea gravel
- Perennial
- Photosynthesis
- Pollination
- Sphagnum moss
- Transplanting
- Ventilation

21ST-CENTURY SKILLS: Critical thinking and problem-solving skills, collaboration skills, flexibility and adaptability, initiative and self-direction, productivity and accountability, leadership and responsibility, interdisciplinary understanding, mastery of core subjects

HELPFUL HINTS:

- Remember that tropical terrariums are damp, and it's important that they are waterproof so that water does not leak out.

- Keep in mind that the size of the container used limits the types of plants that can be used inside the terrarium. Large containers generally are a better option because they give you more flexibility.
- For tropical terrariums, creating a drainage area below the soil or bedding will make it last longer.
- Remember that mixing different species together can be dangerous. So be sure to research what can be combined safely.
- Consider the temperature and light needed by the inhabitants of your terrarium when picking a location for showcasing.

EXEMPLARY PRODUCERS:

- Ron Gladkowski
- Paula Hayes
- Wanda Macnair
- Tovah Martin
- Donna Moramarco
- P. Allen Smith
- Nathaniel Ward

COMMUNITY RESOURCES: Science/botany/ecology teacher, local landscaper, local pet store

BOOK:

Bearce, S. (2009). *A kid's guide to making a terrarium.* Hockessin, DE: Mitchell Lane.

WEB SITE:

Activity: Building a Terrarium
http://www.kidsgardening.com/2006.kids.garden.news/jan/pg3.html
Provides directions on constructing your own terrarium.

QUOTE TO INSPIRE:

"My garden will never make me famous, I'm a horticultural ignoramus."—Ogden Nash

TERRARIUM PRODUCT GUIDE	
COMPONENTS	EXEMPLARY CHARACTERISTICS
Appearance	• Realistic, contoured landscape • Attractive use of accents (i.e., stone, wood, etc.)
Construction	• Neat, attractive • Follows plans accurately • Durable, withstands common stressors
Function	• Functions extraordinarily well • Plants and/or animals thrive
Journal (Optional)	• Complete, detailed record of observations • Includes corresponding pictures/drawings
Plan/Diagram	• Neat • Clear measurements • All components are clearly labeled • Creates a well-balanced, sustainable ecosystem • Compatible plants and/or animals are selected with respect to lighting, watering, and humidity needs • Contains a complete list of materials needed for construction • Consideration given for proper drainage

PRODUCT: TESSELLATION

DEFINITION: A repeated pattern resulting from the arrangement of regular polygons that cover a plane without any gaps or overlaps.

....

TITLES OF THE EXPERT: Artist, mathematician

....

TYPES OF TESSELLATIONS:

- Aperiodic
- Asymmetric
- Fractal
- Irregular
- Periodic
- Regular
- Semiregular
- Symmetric

....

WORDS TO KNOW:

- Angle
- Congruent
- Equilateral triangle
- Heptagon
- Hexagon
- Octagon
- Pentagon
- Polygon
- Reflection
- Rotation
- Symmetry
- Tessella
- Tiling
- Trapezoid
- Vertex

....

21ST-CENTURY SKILLS: Creativity and innovation skills, critical thinking and problem-solving skills, technology skills, flexibility and adaptability, productivity and accountability, interdisciplinary understanding, mastery of core subjects

....

HELPFUL HINTS:
- Use grid paper to ensure your shapes are uniform.
- Regular pentagons will not tessellate, but there are 14 known 5-sided shapes that will.
- There are only three regular tessellations: triangles, squares, and hexagons.
- A vertex is just a "corner point," or the point where adjacent shapes meet.
- To name a tessellation, go around a vertex and write down how many sides each polygon has, in order, and always start at the polygon with the least number of sides.

EXEMPLARY PRODUCERS:

- M. C. Escher
- Robert Fathauer
- E. S. Fedorov
- Michael Hirschhorn
- Johannes Kepler
- K. E. Landry
- Sol LeWitt
- Roger Penrose
- Marjorie Rice
- Bridget Louise Riley
- Victor Vasarely
- Hans Voderberg

COMMUNITY RESOURCES: Math/art teacher, college professors

BOOKS:

Roza, G. (2005). *An optical artist: Exploring patterns and symmetry.* New York: PowerKids Press.

Stephens, P., & McNeill, J. (2001). *Tessellations: The history and making of symmetrical designs.* Aspen, CO: Crystal Productions.

WEB SITE:

CoolMath4Kids.com—Tessellations
http://www.coolmath4kids.com/tesspag1.html
Overview of tessellations with supporting images.

QUOTES TO INSPIRE:

"By keenly confronting the enigmas that surround us, and by considering and analyzing the observations that I have made, I ended up in the domain of mathematics. Although I am absolutely without training in the exact sciences, I often seem to have more in common with mathematicians than with my fellow artists."—M. C. Escher

"Talent and all that are really for the most part just baloney. Any schoolboy with a little aptitude can perhaps draw better than I; but what he lacks in most cases is that tenacious desire to make it reality, that obstinate gnashing of teeth and saying, 'Although I know it can't be done, I want to do it anyway.'"—M. C. Escher

TESSELLATION PRODUCT GUIDE	
COMPONENTS	EXEMPLARY CHARACTERISTICS
Appearance/Design/ Pattern	• Compositionally challenging, intricate • Appropriate emphasis of shape or subject • Design elements (i.e., color, balance, unity, symmetry, etc.) are comprehensively executed • Pattern is consistently neat and precise throughout • Evidence of preplanning
Craftsmanship	• Carefully crafted, clean and neat • Unified pattern, complete and accurate, parts fit together tightly with no gaps or overlaps • Superior use of space, coverage of entire plane • Demonstrates a clear understanding of tessellations

PRODUCT: TIME CAPSULE

DEFINITION: A sealed container for preserving and archiving contemporary, culturally relevant records and items with the intent of being opened and analyzed in the future.

TITLES OF THE EXPERT: Archivist, historian, archeologist, objects conservator

TYPES OF TIME CAPSULES:
- Intentional
- Unintentional

WORDS TO KNOW:
- Anthropology
- Archive
- Artifacts
- Deteriorate
- Ephemera
- Future
- Generation
- Keepsake
- Memorabilia
- Polyethylene
- Preservation

21ST-CENTURY SKILLS: Creativity and innovation skills, critical thinking and problem-solving skills, communication skills, collaboration skills, media literacy, flexibility and adaptability, social and cross-cultural skills, leadership and responsibility, interdisciplinary understanding, mastery of core subjects

HELPFUL HINTS:
- Keep in mind that time capsules do not have to be buried. In fact, depending on the type of container used, storing them above ground may better preserve the contents.
- Black-and-white photos will not fade as much as colored photos, so use the former when possible.
- Have family members include letters to the older versions of themselves or to future generations.
- Avoid including CD-ROMs or DVDs as these forms of technology may be obsolete in the future, and the data on such storage devices may be unreadable in the future.
- Newspapers deteriorate rapidly. Consider photocopying selected articles onto acid-free paper to ensure adequate preservation.

EXEMPLARY PRODUCERS:

- Thornwell Jacobs
- William Jarvis
- George Edward Pendray
- Andy Warhol
- George Washington

COMMUNITY RESOURCES: History teacher, professor of anthropology, librarian

BOOKS:

Caney, S. (1991). *Make your own time capsule.* New York: Workman.

Forrester, T., & Shapiro, S. (1999). *Create your own millennium time capsule.* Toronto: Annick Press.

Packard, M. (1999). *Make your own time capsule.* Mahwah, NJ: Troll.

Seibert, P. (2002). *We were here: A short history of time capsules.* Brookfield, CT: Millbrook Press.

WEB SITES

International Time Capsule Society
http://www.oglethorpe.edu/about_us/crypt_of_civilization/international_time_capsule_society.asp
Organization established to promote the careful study of time capsules.

State Library and Archives of Florida—Making Time Capsules
http://dlis.dos.state.fl.us/archives/preservation/time
Overview of the many considerations when creating a time capsule.

QUOTE TO INSPIRE:

"We seem to have a compulsion these days to bury time capsules in order to give those people living in the next century or so some idea of what we are like."—Alfred Hitchcock

TIME CAPSULE PRODUCT GUIDE	
COMPONENTS	EXEMPLARY CHARACTERISTICS
Container	• Appropriately labeled • Visually appealing • Selected in consideration for the preservation of artifacts
Contents/Artifacts	• Carefully selected, relevant to theme/purpose • Authentic • Prepared in a manner that enhances preservation • Well-organized
Support/Documentation	• Detailed description of each artifact and thorough justification of its inclusion in the capsule • Correct spelling and grammar

PRODUCT: TRAVELOGUE

DEFINITION: A film or illustrated lecture on traveling.

TITLE OF THE EXPERT: Travel writer

TYPES OF TRAVELOGUES:

- Essay
- Fictional
- Guidebook
- Itinerary
- Journal
- Nature

WORDS TO KNOW:

- Anecdote
- Atmosphere
- Attractions
- Byline
- Chronological
- Conquest
- Culture
- Destination
- Foreign
- Itinerary
- Journey
- Locals
- Narrative
- Nonfiction
- Ship's log
- Tourism

21ST-CENTURY SKILLS: Creativity and innovation skills, communication skills, technology skills, flexibility and adaptability, initiative and self-direction, social and cross-cultural skills, productivity and accountability, interdisciplinary understanding, mastery of core subjects

HELPFUL HINTS:

- Incorporate photographs of the places you visit to accompany your narrative.
- Be descriptive; consider all of your senses when writing about a place or experience, so the reader feels like he or she is there too.
- Establish a particular time of the day that you will write, so it becomes routine.
- Always proofread carefully.

EXEMPLARY PRODUCERS:

- Matsuo Bashō
- Hilaire Belloc
- James Boswell
- Sally Carrighar
- William Clark
- Charles Darwin
- Charles Dickens
- Gerald Durrell
- Johann Wolfgang von Goethe
- Che Guevara
- William Least Heat-Moon
- Samuel Johnson
- Jon Krakauer
- Charles Kuralt
- D. H. Lawrence
- Meriwether Lewis
- David Livingstone
- Jan Morris
- Eric Newby
- Kira Salak
- Ivan T. Sanderson
- Ernest Shackleton
- John Steinbeck
- Robert Louis Stevenson
- Rick Steves
- Paul Theroux
- Evelyn Waugh
- Rebecca West

COMMUNITY RESOURCES: English/writing teacher, college English professor

BOOK:

Bree, L. G., & Bree, M. (2007). *Kid's trip diary.* St. Paul, MN: Marlor Press.

WEB SITES:

Momsminivan.com—Making Memories: Creating a Travel Journal for Kids
http://www.momsminivan.com/tripjournal.html
An author shares travel journals created by her children.

Discovering Lewis and Clark
http://www.lewis-clark.org/content/content-journals.asp
Read excerpts from this famous travel journal.

QUOTE TO INSPIRE:

"The great thing about travel books is that they are written with a voice, but sometimes it's hard to deliver that voice with real personality. With travel advice, you want to feel like you're getting it from a good friend. You know, the inside scoop."—Larry Olson

TRAVELOGUE
PRODUCT GUIDE

Components	Exemplary Characteristics
Appearance	• Visually pleasing, attractive • Easy to read • Appropriate design for content/theme/mood
Entries	• Informative, accurate information is presented • Clear reasoning/rationale for including specific information • Interesting, engages readers with appropriately selected anecdotes • Descriptive; uses vivid language; consideration to all senses when describing setting, people, and/or events • Well-organized, logical sequence of events
Mechanics	• Appropriate use of grammar • Well-constructed paragraphs • Free of spelling errors • Strong evidence of proofreading
Photos/Illustrations (Optional)	• Neat, visually appealing • Enhance reader's understanding

PRODUCT: VIDEO GAME

DEFINITION: A software program typically displayed on a computer, television, console, or handheld device in which one or more players make decisions and control various game objects and resources in pursuit of a goal.

TITLES OF THE EXPERT: Software engineer, gamer

TYPES OF VIDEO GAMES:

- Action
- Action-Adventure
- Adventure
- Arcade
- Driving/Racing
- Educational
- Multiplayer
- Music/Dance
- Puzzle
- Role-play
- Sandbox
- Simulation
- Sports
- Strategy
- Three-dimensional
- Trivia
- Two-dimensional

WORDS TO KNOW:

- Backwards compatibility
- BitBlt
- C++
- Cheats
- Code
- Console
- Controller
- Design
- DirectX
- Glitch
- Hardware
- JAVA
- Joystick
- OpenGL
- Peripheral
- Pixel
- Platform
- Programming
- Screen
- Software
- Spoiler
- Strategy
- Tactic
- User interface
- WiFi

21ST-CENTURY SKILLS: Creativity and innovation skills, critical thinking and problem-solving skills, communication skills, collaboration skills, technology skills, media literacy, flexibility and adaptability, initiative and self-direction, productivity and accountability, leadership and responsibility, interdisciplinary understanding, mastery of core subjects

HELPFUL HINTS:

- Think of an idea for your game. You will need to create a main character, a setting, a plot, and a theme just as you would for a regular story.

- Create backgrounds for your game world, including character studies, historical information, geographic descriptions, and back stories for everything important to your game world.
- To organize how your game will play out at different points along the way, write up a flowchart that traces all possible pathways and decisions of the various characters throughout the entire game.
- Write out a detailed script of your game, including character dialogue, sound effects information, and any other details you want to include.

EXEMPLARY PRODUCERS:

- Scott Adams
- Ralph H. Baer
- Danielle Bunten Berry
- Ed Boon
- Nolan Bushnell
- John D. Carmack
- Ted Dabney
- Alexander S. Douglas
- Thomas T. Goldsmith, Jr.
- Martin Graetz
- William Higinbotham
- Estle Ray Mann
- Jordan Mechner
- Sidney K. Meier
- Alan Miller
- Rand Miller
- Robyn Miller
- Peter Douglas Molyneux
- Steve Russell
- Chris Sawyer
- Ken Silverman
- Tim Sweeney
- Anne Westfall
- Wayne Wiitanen
- Don Woods
- William Wright

COMMUNITY RESOURCES: Computer teacher, local software engineer

BOOK:

Pratchett, R. (2008). *Video games*. New York: Crabtree.

WEB SITES:

Steve Tutes—Java for Kids
http://www.video-animation.com/java_000.shtml
Tutorial for designing a basic video game.

Scratch
http://scratch.mit.edu
A new programming language that makes it easy to create interactive stories, animations, games, music, and art.

QUOTES TO INSPIRE:
"Video games are bad for you? That's what they said about rock and roll."—Shigeru Miyamoto

"I recently learned something quite interesting about video games. Many young people have developed incredible hand, eye, and brain coordination in playing these games. The Air Force believes these kids will be our outstanding pilots should they fly our jets."—Ronald Reagan

VIDEO GAME PRODUCT GUIDE	
COMPONENTS	EXEMPLARY CHARACTERISTICS
Concept/Goal/Strategy	• Establishes a clear goal, both short-term and long-term goals are considered to keep players motivated • Appropriately challenging, varying degrees of difficulty • Presents player with interesting decisions that enhance game play • Engaging and/or enjoyable for the player
Design/Interface	• Creates an illusion of depth/space in support of game design • Images create a desired atmosphere or tone • Original and interesting characters • Logically organized • Strong awareness of audience in the design • Easy-to-use buttons and attractive displays
Programming/Code	• Easy to read and well-documented • Demonstrates solid knowledge of code/programming language • Appropriate for game strategy
Rules/Instructions	• Carefully developed • Consider all aspects of the game
Storyboard	• Professional, reflects outstanding planning and organization • Clear • Complete, sketches for each scene • Detailed notes on titles, transitions, special effects, sound, etc.

PRODUCT: WEBQUEST

DEFINITION: An inquiry-based learning activity in which most of the information that a learner interacts with is located on the Internet.

....

TITLE OF THE EXPERT: Information scientist

....

TYPES OF WEBQUESTS:
- Short term
- Long term

....

WORDS TO KNOW:
- Conclusion
- Evaluation
- Hyperlink
- Interdisciplinary
- Internet
- Introduction
- Resources
- Role-play
- Task
- URL
- Videoconferencing
- World Wide Web

....

21ST-CENTURY SKILLS: Creativity and innovation skills, critical thinking and problem-solving skills, communication skills, collaboration skills, technology skills, media literacy, flexibility and adaptability, initiative and self-direction, social and cross-cultural skills, productivity and accountability, leadership and responsibility, interdisciplinary understanding, mastery of core subjects

....

HELPFUL HINTS:
- Locate quality Web Sites. Evaluate sites by carefully reading through all of the linked information and considering the source or author.
- Take time to learn how to use the advanced search techniques available on search engines, such as Google, Yahoo, and AltaVista.
- Good quality information on the Internet is located in the "hidden Web" or pages not found by search engines, such as large databases and library resources like the Library of Congress. Research how to find the URL's for these sites.
- Save what you find by copying and pasting Web site addresses into a Word document or by using free bookmarking sites.

EXEMPLARY PRODUCERS:

- Bernie Dodge
- Kate Fannon
- Annette Lamb
- Tom March
- Dan McDowell
- Jamie McKenzie
- Philip Molebash

COMMUNITY RESOURCES: Computer teacher, Web site developer

BOOKS:

Cook, C. H., & Pfeifer, J. M. (2000). *Internet quest: 101 adventures around the World Wide Web.* Nashville, TN: Incentive Publications.

Pedersen, T., & Moss, F. (2000). *How to find almost anything on the Internet: A kid's guide to safe searching.* New York: Price Stern Sloan.

WEB SITES:

WebQuest.org
http://www.webquest.org
Find, create, and share WebQuests.

A WebQuest About WebQuests
http://webquest.sdsu.edu/webquestwebquest-es.html
Suggestions for evaluating potential sites to include in a WebQuest.

QUOTE TO INSPIRE:

"Be an explorer . . . read, surf the Internet, visit customers, enjoy arts, watch children play . . . do anything to prevent yourself from becoming a prisoner of your knowledge, experience, and current view of the world."—Charles Thompson

WEBQUEST PRODUCT GUIDE	
COMPONENTS	EXEMPLARY CHARACTERISTICS
Information Sources/ Resources	• Incorporates a variety of information sources (i.e., Web documents, experts available via e-mail or conferencing, searchable databases, books and/or other documents) • Includes accurate pointers/links to resources
Introduction	• Sets the stage • Provides sufficient background information • Engages and excites learner • Provides learner with a role to play (i.e., scientist, detective, reporter) • Presents task within the context of an inviting scenario (i.e., You've been asked by the CIA . . .)
Process	• Clearly described • Separated into individual steps • Incorporates varied and clear guidelines regarding how to organize the information acquired (i.e., guiding questions, timelines, concept maps, or cause-and-effect diagrams)
Summary/Conclusion	• Satisfying • Incorporates review, reminds the learner about what he or she has learned • Fosters connections, encourages learner to extend the experience into other domains • Encourages reflection
Task	• Doable • Interesting and fun • Visually and aesthetically appealing • Meaningful and/or important (e.g., global warming, acid rain, poverty, etc.)

PRODUCTS AND COMPETITIONS

Competitions are another great venue for the various products that students create. Whether the product is an animation or illustrated story, there are many contests designed specifically for school-aged children.

Aside from creating a wider audience for the product, there are many other benefits to participating in competitions. These include, but are not limited to:

- reinforcing time management strategies;
- enhancing self-confidence;
- networking with others; and,
- receiving scholarships, cash, trophies, ribbons, certificates, travel, and other fun prizes.

There are several ways to obtain information on competitions. Teachers, guidance counselors, administrators, curriculum coordinators, librarians, and media specialists among others may have information regarding a wide array of competitions. Youth magazines, newspapers, and Web sites may be other places where competitions are announced. A basic Internet search for "kids and competitions" will generate hundreds of hits. Such searches can be further narrowed by adding the product type and/or subject area (i.e., "poetry competitions for kids" or "science competitions for students").

Some competitions may be a one-time event, while others are held annually. Whatever the case, it is important to carefully read the competition's guidelines to determine deadlines, restrictions, and eligibility criteria.

Following is a list of competitions that may be of interest. For other ideas consult the book, *Competitions for Talented Kids* by Frances A. Karnes and Tracy L Riley (2005).

An Artistic Discovery: The Congressional Art Competition
http://www.house.gov/house/ArtGuidelines.shtml
Ages/Grades: High school students
Prize: Work displayed in U.S. Capitol Building for one year
Product: Paintings, drawings, collage, prints, mixed media, computer-generated art, photography

Doodle 4 Google
http://www.google.com/doodle4google
Ages/Grades: Grades K–12
Prize: College scholarship funds, laptop computer, T-shirt, design featured on Google Web site for 24 hours, and a technology grant for school's computer lab
Product: Visual arts and creative writing

First Freedom Student Essay Competition
http://www.firstfreedom.org/education/students.html
Ages/Grades: Grades 9–12
Prize: Cash award
Product: Essay

I'd Rather Be Video Contest
http://www.giantcampus.com/Community/video-contest
Ages/Grades: Ages 10–17
Prize: Free week at any Giant Campus Tech, Digital Media, and Gaming Camp
Product: Video

International Student Media Festival
http://www.ismf.net/ns
Ages/Grades: All ages
Prize: Medal, trophy, cash prize for school
Product: Video, Web site, animation, podcast, photograph, photo essay, sequential stills, interactive stills

Invent a Game
http://www.bkfk.com/games
Ages/Grades: Ages 5–19
Prize: U.S. Savings Bond, game produced by EA Games
Product: Idea for a video game

Kid's Science Challenge
http://www.kidsciencechallenge.com
Ages/Grades: Grades 3–6
Prize: Selection of science toys/kits, trips
Product: An original question, problem, or experiment that relates to four fields of scientific inquiry or engineering

The Lions International Peace Poster
http://www.lionsclubs.org
Ages/Grades: Ages 11–13
Prize: Money and trip
Product: Poster

National Geographic Kids Hands-On Explorer Challenge
http://kids.nationalgeographic.com
Ages/Grades: Ages 9–14
Prize: 12-day expedition
Product: Photo essay

National Kids-in-Print Contest
http://www.landmarkeditions.com/Scripts/contest.asp
Ages/Grades: Ages 6–19
Prize: Cash scholarship to be applied to an accredited college, university, or institute of higher learning
Product: Illustrated book

The PTA's Reflection Program
http://www.pta.org
Ages/Grades: Grades Pre-K–12
Prize: Money, trip, and medallion
Product: Film/video production, dance choreography, musical composition, photography, visual arts, and literature

Scholastic Art & Writing Awards
http://www.artandwriting.org
Ages/Grades: Grades 7–12
Prize: Medals/certificates, celebration at Carnegie Hall, scholarships, and exhibition/publication of work
Product: Visual arts and creative writing

TOYchallenge
http://www.sallyridescience.com/toychallenge
Ages/Grades: Grades 5–8
Prize: Roundtrip flight anywhere in U.S., medal/trophy
Product: Toy

Young Composer's Challenge
http://www.youngcomposerschallenge.com
Ages/Grades: Ages 13–18 in Southeastern U.S.
Prize: Cash and the winning piece will be performed by the Orlando Philharmonic Orchestra in a public concert at the Bob Carr Performing Arts Center
Product: Orchestral composition/original score

CHAPTER 6

PRODUCT JOURNAL

The following pages have been provided to organize product development in the classroom and cultivate purposeful reflection throughout the production process. Both are essential in ensuring a successful experience for students.

Planning and organizational strategies help students self-regulate their learning. Assigning students a significant role in monitoring their own progress fosters engagement, encourages independence, and increases student accountability in creative product development.

Reflection is an important component of any learning experience and lends itself particularly well to product development and evaluation. Careful reflection facilitates critical thinking and helps students make connections between the product, the process of developing it, and their world. Embedding focused reflection into all phases of product development enhances metacognition, thus helping students to realize all they have learned throughout the process. Reflection also fosters student growth and enhances future product development.

Name: _____ Date: _____

PRODUCT PROFILE

The product profiles contained within this book should not be considered all-inclusive. If other products are discovered, information pertaining to them can be noted using the format below.

Product:	
Definition: Describes the product	
Title of the Expert: Job titles of the professionals who create this product	
Types of _____: Examples of various types of the product (i.e., for a map, examples might be relief, topographic, globe, etc.)	
Words to Know: Terms associated with the product that might be used by professionals creating the product	
21st-Century Skills: List of skills that are developed while creating this product	
Helpful Hints: Statements of advice professionals might offer to students who create this product	
Exemplary Producers: Specific individuals who are recognized for expertise in this product	
Community Resources: People and places that students might locate within their community to learn more about the product	
Books: Resource books to expand knowledge with regard to this product	
Web Sites: Internet sites to expand knowledge with regard to this product	
Quotes to Inspire: Quotes related to the product.	

WHY I WANT TO DEVELOP AND EVALUATE MY PRODUCT

There may be many great reasons for developing and evaluating a product. Record as many as you can now and add to the list as you think of more.

1. _____

2. _____

3. _____

4. _____

5. _____

6. _____

7. _____

8. _____

9. _____

10. _____

11. _____

12. _____

13. _____

14. _____

15. _____

16. _____

17. _____

18. _____

19. _____

20. _____

MY PRODUCT GOALS

What are your product goals? What skills in product development would you like to enhance? With whom would you like to meet and share your ideas? Product development can lead to the accomplishment of many personal goals. Think about your goals and how you plan to achieve them through product development. Record them below.

Goal: _____

Steps to achieving my goal:

1. _____

2. _____

3. _____

4. _____

5. _____

Goal: _____

Steps to achieving my goal:

1. _____

2. _____

3. _____

4. _____

5. _____

Name: _____ Date: _____

MY PRODUCT CALENDAR

Having and maintaining a schedule for developing and evaluating your product is very important. You may want to record your schedule on your computer, or perhaps you have a desk or pocket calendar. You also can use the blank calendar below.

Day of the Week	Things to Do Today
Monday	
Tuesday	
Wednesday	
Thursday	
Friday	
Saturday	
Sunday	

Name: _____ Date: _____

MATERIALS FOR MY PRODUCT

As you begin to think about your product, you will have to assess materials and other resources. Which materials do you have? Which ones will you need to acquire? Where will you get these materials? Use the graphic organizer below to keep track of this information.

Materials I Have	Materials I Need	Where to Get Them

PLACES I'VE DISPLAYED MY PRODUCT

There are many places within your school and community to present and/or display your products. Keeping a record will help you remember the details for future exhibitions.

Date	Product	Location

PRODUCT SELECTION:
WHY I DID WHAT I DID!

Reflect upon the process you went through in order to select a product to develop. What elements of the following criteria contributed to your choice of product? Describe.

PERSONAL INTERESTS	
TALENTS AND ABILITIES	
AVAILABLE RESOURCES	
CONTENT	
OTHER	

The Ultimate Guide for Student Product Development & Evaluation (2nd ed.)

Name: _____ Date: _____

WHAT I HAVE LEARNED ABOUT MYSELF WHILE DEVELOPING PRODUCTS

Product development can teach you a lot of things about yourself, your interests, your strengths, and your abilities. You can learn more about your work habits, attitudes, and goals for the future as you plan your product.

Through product development, I have learned the following about my:

INTERESTS 👍	ATTITUDES ☺
STRENGTHS ⍦	WORK HABITS 📁
ABILITIES ⚡	RESEARCH SKILLS 🔍
PRESENTATION SKILLS 🗣	TIME MANAGEMENT 🕐

Name: _____ Date: _____

THE THRILL OF DEVELOPING PRODUCTS

Think about the thrill of gaining new knowledge and transforming the information into a product. How do you feel or think you will feel before, during, and after developing a product? Record these feelings.

WHEN THINKING ABOUT AND DEVELOPING MY PRODUCT, I MAY FEEL OR HAVE FELT . . .

DURING THE DEVELOPMENT OF MY PRODUCT, I MAY FEEL OR HAVE FELT . . .

AFTER COMPLETING MY PRODUCT, I MAY FEEL OR HAVE FELT . . .

THINGS I CAN DO IN DEVELOPING PRODUCTS IN THE FUTURE TO ENCOURAGE POSITIVE FEELINGS INCLUDE . . .

Name: _____ Date: _____

PRODUCTS I WOULD LIKE
TO TRY IN THE FUTURE

Keep a list of the different types of products you would like to create. Be sure to explore a wide variety of products.

VISUAL PRODUCTS *Those products that communicate ideas and knowledge through a variety of media and emphasize sight and space as the primary mode of learning.*	
WRITTEN PRODUCTS *Those products that record ideas and knowledge through writing and composition.*	
ORAL PRODUCTS *Those products that rely solely on verbal, spoken, and unwritten means of communicating knowledge.*	
PERFORMANCE PRODUCTS *Those products that communicate through action, movement, and execution, emphasizing kinesthetic integration.*	
MULTICATEGORICAL PRODUCTS *Those products that combine two or more of the above categories.*	

HAVING FUN WITH PRODUCT DEVELOPMENT THROUGH COMPETITIONS

There are many opportunities for you to share your products through competitions. Competitions exist at the local, state, national, and international levels. Duplicate this form and use it to record information on the competitions that you discover.

Name of Competition:	
Sponsoring Organization:	
Web Site:	
Contact Information:	
Deadline:	
Eligibility Information:	
Award:	
Notes:	

Name of Competition:	
Sponsoring Organization:	
Web Site:	
Contact Information:	
Deadline:	
Eligibility Information:	
Award:	
Notes:	

Name: _____ Date: _____

GREATEST PRODUCT DEVELOPERS
HALL OF FAME

Who would you nominate as the greatest developer of a specific product? Record your nominations below and defend your selections.

Product:	
Nominee:	
Reasons for Nomination:	

Product:	
Nominee:	
Reasons for Nomination:	

Product:	
Nominee:	
Reasons for Nomination:	

REFERENCES

Baker, E. L., & Schacter J. (1996). Expert benchmarks for student academic performance: The case for gifted children. *Gifted Child Quarterly, 40,* 61–65.

Byrnes, P., & Parke, B. (1982, April). *Creative Products Scale: Detroit public schools.* Paper presented at the annual meeting of the Council for Exceptional Children, Houston, TX. (ERIC Document Reproduction No. ED218903)

Costa, A. L., & Kallick, B. (2000). *Habits of mind: A developmental series.* Alexandria, VA: Association for Supervision and Curriculum Development.

Dewey, J. (1933). *How we think: A restatement of the relation of reflective thinking to the educative process.* Boston: D. C. Heath.

Forster, B. R. (1990). Let's build a sailboat: A differentiated gifted education project. *Teaching Exceptional Children, 22*(4), 40–42.

Gibbons, M. (1991). *How to become an expert: Discover, research, and build a project in your chosen field.* Tucson, AZ: Zephyr Press.

Karnes, F. A., & Riley, T. L. (2005). *Competitions for talented kids: Win scholarships, big prize money, and recognition.* Waco, TX: Prufrock Press.

Kettle, K. E., Renzulli, J. S., & Rizza, M. G. (1998). Products of mind: Exploring student preferences for product development using My Way . . . An Expression Style Inventory. *Gifted Child Quarterly, 42,* 49–60.

Maker, J. C., & Nielson, A. B. (1996). *Curriculum development and teaching strategies for gifted learners* (2nd ed.). Austin, TX: PRO-ED.

National Council for the Social Studies. (1994). *Expectations of excellence: Curriculum standards for social studies.* Washington, DC: Author. Retrieved from http://www.socialstudies.org/standards/introduction

National Council of Teachers of English. (1996). *Standards for the English language arts.* Newark, DE: International Reading Association. Retrieved from http://www.ncte.org/library/NCTEFiles/Resources/Books/Sample/StandardsDoc.pdf

National Council of Teachers of Mathematics. (2000). *Principles and standards for school mathematics*. Reston, VA: Author. Retrieved from http://standards.nctm.org/document/chapter2/learn.htm

National Research Council. (1996). *National Science Education Standards: Observe, interact, change, learn*. Washington, DC: National Academy Press.

Neihart, M. (1999). Systematic risk-taking. *Roeper Review, 21*, 289–293.

Renzulli, J. S., & Reis, S. M. (1991). Building advocacy through program design, student productivity, and public relations. *Gifted Child Quarterly, 35*, 182–187.

Renzulli, J. S., Reis, S. M., & Smith, L. H. (1981). *The Revolving Door Identification Model*. Mansfield Center, CT: Creative Learning Press.

Stephens, K. R., & Karnes, F. A. (2009). Product development for gifted students. In F. A. Karnes & S. M. Bean (Eds.), *Methods and materials for teaching the gifted* (pp. 157–186). Waco, TX: Prufrock Press.

Wiggins, G. (1996). Anchoring assessment with exemplars: Why students and teachers need models. *Gifted Child Quarterly, 40*, 66–69.

Wiggins, G., & McTighe, J. (2005). *Understanding by design*. Alexandria, VA: Association for Supervision and Curriculum Development.

Wikipedia. (2007). *Wikipedia: About*. Retrieved March 24, 2009, from http://en.wikipedia.org/wiki/Wikipedia:About

ABOUT THE AUTHORS

Frances Karnes is professor and director of the Frances A. Karnes Center for Gifted Studies at the University of Southern Mississippi (USM). She also directs the Leadership Studies Program and is widely known for her research, innovative programs, and leadership training. She is author or coauthor of more than 200 published papers and is coauthor of 43 books and has three new books in production. Her work often is cited as the authority on gifted children and the law. She is extensively involved in university activities and civic and professional organizations in the community. Her honors include: Faculty Research Award, Honorary Doctorate from Quincy University, Mississippi Legislature Award for Academic Excellence in Higher Education, USM Professional Service Award, USM Basic Research Award, Rotary International Jean Harris Award, Woman of Achievement Award from the Hattiesburg Women's Forum, Distinguished Alumni Award from the University of Illinois, and Lifetime Innovation Award from the University of Southern Mississippi. The Board of Trustees of Mississippi Institutions of Higher Learning honored her by naming the research, instructional, and service center she founded at USM the Frances A. Karnes Center for Gifted Studies.

Kristen R. Stephens is assistant professor of the practice in the Program in Education at Duke University where she directs the Early Childhood Education Studies Certificate Program and serves as clinical director of the Academically/Intellectually Gifted Licensure Program. She is the coauthor and coeditor of several books, book chapters, and series pertaining to gifted child education.